Quilt BIG

◢ BIGGER BLOCKS FOR FASTER FINISHES ◣

JEMIMA FLENDT

the
Quilting
company

Published by The Quilting Company, an imprint of F+W Media, Inc., 10151 Carver Road, Suite 300, Blue Ash, Ohio 45242. First Edition.

fw

www.fwcommunity.com

The Quilting company

www.quiltingcompany.com

22 21 20 19 18 5 4 3 2 1

SRN: R7240
ISBN-13: 978-1-4402-4854-2

Editorial Director:
KERRY BOGERT

Editor:
JODI BUTLER

Technical Editor:
DEBRA FEHR GREENWAY

Art Director & Designer:
ASHLEE WADESON

Illustrator:
MISSY SHEPLER

Photographer:
GEORGE BOE

DEDICATION

To my girls, Shayla and Ashlyn—you inspire me to show you how hard work and dedication will lead to making your dreams come true.

CONTENTS

INTRODUCTION:

It's funny how life turns out. I never dreamed that one day I would pursue my hobby as a full-time profession. I started quilting when I was about 16 and sewing even before then. I never imagined that my "work day" would look the way it does today.

I know now that my teaching background plays a huge role in my professional quilting career. I have a passion for teaching others how to sew and quilt, and especially enjoy introducing new people to a love of fabric and textiles. I like that I get to travel to teach and host quilting workshops. Accepting and embracing my identity in the quilting industry has let me find my niche and where I fit in.

Writing my first book, *Weekend Quilting*, was a dream come true, made real only by lots of hard work and persistence. There was a steep learning curve as I not only designed the quilts but also discovered how best to communicate patterns to readers, especially beginners. *Quilt Big* brought new challenges, and I learned even more about quilting and writing along the way. Ultimately I wanted to write a book that would help new and experienced quilters alike "quilt better."

In *Quilt Big*, I have taken traditional blocks and sized them up for a gigantic, bold look. With these designs, you can make even a short amount of time productive and satisfying by making progress on big blocks with fast finishes that showcase some of your favorite fabrics. It's all about taking your quilting to the next level, whether you are a beginner or have previous experience. Life is so full and busy these days for everyone, it can be challenging to make time for a hobby. The projects in *Quilt Big* feature a variety of techniques to help you hone your skills and because of their larger size, you'll have them finished in no time.

I also included information to help you figure out the quilt math and see how easy it can be to make changes or modifications. Additionally, I added a variety of quilt-back designs so you can make the back of your quilt as much of a statement piece as the top. There are also suggestions for how to use leftover pieces from the quilt top or fabrics in your stash to make your quilt totally reversible and loveable from either side.

Whether you want to make these projects as special hand-made gifts, to spruce up a spot on your couch, or simply for yourself, you will see how quickly and easily these blocks come together to make stunning and treasured quilts, pillows, and runners.

Happy quilting!

Jemima

CHAPTER 1

QUILTING BASICS

TOOLS AND TECHNIQUES FOR QUILTING ON A GRAND SCALE

When it comes to quilting, bigger can certainly be better! Not only on trend, scaling up pattern designs can make for faster finishes. This book takes the inherent beauty found in single-block patterns and creates big, bold quilts, quickly and easily. What better way to learn the basics of piecing blocks or showcasing your favorite prints than by learning on a grand scale? The bonus: A complete quilt can be made in a matter of days rather than committing months to a single project.

Quilt blocks form the basis of most designs in this book. They take us back to the very heart of quilting with block designs that date back generations and can help you develop your skills and learn new techniques. In this book, we are looking at close to two dozen blocks and how we can use them to create supersized quilt patterns. While most of these blocks date back to the origins of quilting, you will see why they hold just as much relevance in quilting today.

Basic Tools & Supplies

- Sewing machine with ¼" (6 mm) foot
- Additional machine feet, such as a zipper foot, will also be helpful
- Machine sewing needles
- Hand sewing needles for handquilting and binding
- Curved safety pins
- Rotary cutter and self-healing cutting mat
- Masking tape
- Clear acrylic rulers: 12½" (31.5 cm) square, 12½" (31.5 cm) Half-Square Triangle Square Up Ruler, 6" × 12" (15 cm × 30.5 cm) Flying Geese Square Up Ruler, and 6½" × 24" (16.5 cm × 61 cm) ruler (I like Bloc Loc rulers)
- Scissors
- Erasable fabric marking pens
- Seam ripper
- Pencil
- Iron and ironing board

SEWING MACHINE NEEDLES

For general quilting and sewing projects, I use a Universal size 80 needle. Change your needle every 8 hours of sewing time or for every new quilt top. Having a nice sharp needle will ensure it moves smoothly through your fabrics so that you do not get any snagging, skipping, or pulling.

CUTTING

I like to cut fabrics with a rotary cutter and self-healing cutting mat. These mats are gentle on blades so your blade stays sharper longer. Change your rotary cutter blades often to ensure ease of cutting.

Using large 24" (61 cm) rulers will help you cut the longest lengths possible from your fabric. I have specified Bloc Loc rulers for several projects in this book; investing in them will help you cut more accurately when trimming blocks to size.

FABRIC

I love to use a variety of fabrics, including 100-percent cotton, linen, lawn, denim, chambray, and flannel. Often there may be several different fabric types within a single project. If you are starting out, I recommend sticking with 100-percent cotton patchwork fabric. As your skills grow, you can incorporate other fabrics to add texture and interest to your projects.

◢ Note: All fabric yardage in Quilt Big is based on 42" (106.5 cm) wide fabric. It is important to always check the width of your fabric before you begin cutting. Different companies use different widths for their fabrics so measure first to be sure. If the width of your fabric is not 42" (106.5 cm) you may need to make adjustments to the amount of fabric required.

FABRIC CHOICES

When creating large blocks, there are considerations that need to be made for scale of prints, including large-scale versus small-scale patterns and where each of these works best.

Animal Prints

When you are using prints with patterns such as animals or large flowers, you may need to pay a bit more attention when it comes to cutting. For example, you may cut animal prints in half and then realize that once cut, they may not work as desired. It may require more time to cut your fabrics carefully, but looking at where to cut and envisioning how the cut fabric will look once put together will result in a better finish as you re-piece the cut blocks.

Florals

Floral prints are fantastic for large-scale blocks as you get to really appreciate the work in the design and the artistry of the fabric. Many beautiful large-scale floral prints are now available and will work fabulously for these designs. Just consider the size of the print for the specific project before cutting. If the scale of the print is large and the pattern calls for lots of cut pieces, the florals may look distorted when you cut and re-sew the fabrics. Also, once some of the prints are cut up, the colors may look different than how they appeared as a singular piece of fabric.

◢ *Note: You can use an erasable fabric marker on the back of your fabric to mark where to cut pieces if you want to highlight certain focal prints. This will give you a better idea of what you are cutting and how it may look.*

Busy Prints

Busy prints are excellent for supersized blocks as you can appreciate the patterns in larger areas. Another good idea is to use busier prints as your background fabric as they can provide great contrast to designs that use fewer prints and will give greater impact to your finished quilt.

Solids

Using solid fabrics is a great way to give quilts a big bold look.

Bundles

Fat quarter bundles or 10" (25.5 cm) squares will provide lots of contrast to quilts with coordinating fabrics and are a good starting point if you are not confident at choosing fabrics.

THREAD

Use good quality, 100-percent cotton thread whenever possible. It's frustrating to spend a lot of time making a project only to have the thread let you down by breaking, snapping, or shredding. I prefer to use Aurifil 50wt thread for piecing and machine quilting. For handquilting, I like to use an Aurifil 12wt thread. The colors are amazing, and I can coordinate them for every project.

Tips and Techniques

SEAM ALLOWANCES

Always sew with a ¼" (6 mm) seam allowance. The best way to achieve this is by using a ¼" (6 mm) foot on your sewing machine. Match raw edges together and line up the edge of the fabric with the edge of the machine foot. When all of your seams are the correct size, your pieces should fit together easily and the seams should match up neatly.

WASHING FABRIC

Washing fabric causes much debate among quilters. I don't prewash fabric before I start quilting unless it is a color that may bleed, such as black, red, or navy. If you don't prewash your fabric, adding a color-absorbing laundry sheet when washing your quilt can help take care of any excess dye in the water.

PRESSING

A lot of patterns assume you know how to press and in which direction. Pressing fabric correctly will make for a better-finished quilt top. I have included instructions in this book. Press all fabric before you start. This helps ensure that any shrinkage happens before you cut out your pieces rather than after you have them cut to size. Always try to press fabric on the wrong side.

When setting seams, always press the sewn seam first (before you open the fabrics), then press the fabric in the correct direction. This will allow the stitches to "meld together" and will hold the fabric better. It also helps to alleviate distortion or stretching as you press the seams in one direction or another.

Generally, when you press seams to one side, press them toward the darker fabric. If you are using fabrics that have a white or light background against dark fabrics, it is often best to press seams open to avoid dark shadows.

Putting It All Together

Once you have assembled the top of your quilt or project, it is time to put all the layers together and finish it off. Due to the supersized nature of many of the quilts and projects in this book, the quilting is going to play an important role in the look of your finished project. With larger areas of negative space or background fabrics comes the need to quilt to these spaces to add more interest and detail.

SANDWICH YOUR QUILT

To make a "Quilt Sandwich," lay the backing fabric on the floor right-side down. Smooth out any wrinkles, then hold the fabric in place with masking tape. Lay the batting on top and make sure it is wrinkle free. After pressing the quilt top, lay it over the batting with the right-side up and baste the three layers together with safety pins.

Starting from the center of the quilt sandwich, place the pins about 3" (7.5 cm) apart for hand quilting or 4" (10 cm) apart for machine quilting. Work equally on all sides until you get to the edges (**Figure 1**).

You can also "thread baste" the layers if you prefer. Use long, hand-basting stitches to secure the layers together. Spray basting is another way to baste the layers together.

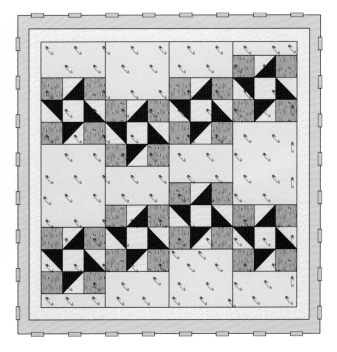

Fig. 1

QUILTING

Machine Quilting

I have used a variety of quilting options for the projects in this book. Some I machine quilted using the designs in the quilt/project tops to inspire the quilting designs. I like straight-line machine quilting and free-motion machine quilting, which I can do on my domestic machine.

Handquilting

This is a real love of mine. I adore the "perfectly imperfect" stitches and the texture it creates in projects, which is quite different from machine quilting. I often handquilt projects that I have handsewn.

Longarm Quilting

I had a number of the larger quilts in this book longarm quilted due to their size. If you choose to have your quilts longarm quilted, you do not need to baste them. Choose designs that reflect your project, and keep in mind that longarm quilting can change the texture of a quilt. Heavier and denser quilting patterns, for example, will stiffen your quilt, while loose patterns allow for a softer drape. I like to choose patterns based on the type of fabric I used or ones that echo the design. You can use a floral pattern with floral fabrics, for example. Geometric patterns are great when these patterns are echoed in the quilt design. If you are unsure what will best suit your quilt, ask your longarm quilter for suggestions.

Washing Quilts

When needed, I wash my quilts with wool wash in a washing machine on a gentle cycle, then reduce the spin cycle to a lower setting. I also throw a color-absorbing laundry sheet in with the quilt to absorb any excess dye in the water so fabrics do not bleed. After a quilt comes out of the washing machine, I hang it on a clothesline from one end with lots of clothespins, rotating it periodically so the quilt dries evenly and does not stretch from the weight of any excess water. Once the quilt is dry, bring it in so it doesn't stay in the elements too long.

CREATING THE BINDING

Binding is the last step in making quilts and projects. It is the finishing touch that can add just the right detail. I prefer to use smaller scale prints for binding as long as the print shows in a narrow width. (I am a big fan of stripe bindings at the moment.) Avoid using prints such as large dots or spots. If you miss the dot print when folding the binding, the dots may appear to drift off the edge or look uneven. Always choose colors or prints that complement your design.

1. To calculate how much binding you will need, measure the length of each side of the quilt. Add the numbers together, then add 10" (25.5 cm) to the total.

2. Join the binding strips by placing 2 strips at right angles. Mark a diagonal line from the top left corner to the bottom right and stitch along this line (**Figure 1**). Trim the corner (**Figure 2**). Press the seams open, then press the entire strip in half lengthwise with wrong sides together (**Figure 3**).

3. Starting about halfway along one side of the quilt and leaving a 6" (15 cm) tail, sew the binding strip to the right side of the quilt, mitering the corners as you go. To miter the corners, stop ¼" (6 mm) before you reach the corner of your quilt. Put the needle down into the quilt at this point and rotate the quilt 90 degrees. Reverse stitch back to the raw edge of

the binding, then place the needle down into the quilt at this raw edge of the binding. Lift up the presser foot. Fold the binding at a 90-degree angle away from the quilt top and back again, covering the angle you created. Line up the raw edges and sew along the next side of your quilt (**Figure 4**). Continue to sew around your quilt.

4. Stop about 6" (15 cm) from where you started. Open both ends of the binding and place the right sides together. Join each binding strip with a diagonal line as you did in step 2. Trim the seam allowance, then continue sewing the binding to the quilt top.

5. Trim the backing and batting, then fold over the binding and slip stitch into place, mitering the corners in the opposite direction from the front corners, along the back seam line (**Figure 5**).

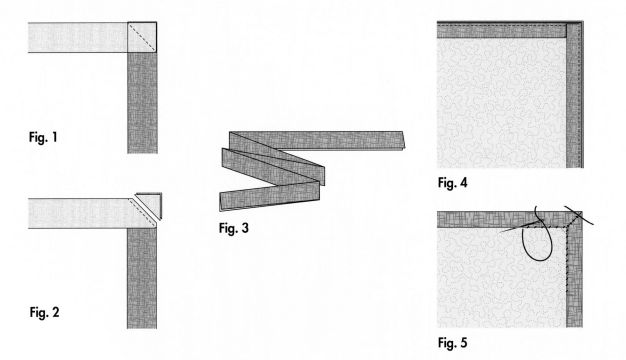

Fig. 1

Fig. 2

Fig. 3

Fig. 4

Fig. 5

CHAPTER 2

UPSIZING QUILTS AND QUILT BLOCKS

As someone who never liked math much in school and wasn't that great at it, I find it ironic just how much math I use for quilting. Whether it is converting inches into centimeters or meters into yards, calculating dimensions, sizing blocks, or working out binding requirements, there is a lot of math involved in designing and creating quilts.

Becoming confident in working out quilting calculations will open up a range of new block patterns and ways to design your own quilts to make them any size you choose. It will also mean you can easily work out fabric requirements for what you need to purchase.

TOOLS YOU NEED:

- Ruler or tape measure
- Lead pencil
- Colored pencils
- Grid paper
- Calculator

COMMON QUILT DIMENSIONS

First, it is important to know the mattress dimensions of different sized beds. This will allow you to work out the size quilt you may need to make.

Common Quilt Sizes

MATTRESS AND LAP SIZES	SUGGESTED QUILT SIZES
Crib **27" × 52"** (68.5 cm × 132 cm)	**36" × 60"** (91.5 cm × 152.5 cm)
Twin **39" × 75"** (99 cm × 190.5 cm)	**70" × 90"** (178 cm × 228.5 cm)
Double (or Full) **54" × 75"** (137 cm × 190.5 cm)	**84" × 90"** (213.5 cm × 228.5 cm)
Queen **60" × 80"** (152.5 cm × 203 cm)	**90" × 95"** (228.5 cm × 241.5 cm)
King **76" × 80"** (193 cm × 203 cm)	**108" × 95"** (274.5 cm × 241.5 cm)
Lap **Sizes vary**	**59"** (150 cm) square

Upsizing Quilt Blocks

RESIZING GRIDS

Deciding to upsize a quilt pattern can be as easy as adding or making additional blocks or borders. This is an easy option for achieving a larger size quilt and is great if you are not as confident working out the quilt math. But what if you want to upsize the scale of the blocks in a pattern? Once you get the hang of it, it is fairly easy. Here is how you do it.

Frequently, blocks are made up from a grid formation. When you take a block and divide it into a grid, you will more easily see how to work out resizing blocks.

NINE PATCH

Let's use the Simplex Star block in chapter 3 as an example. You can see by dividing up this block that it is made up of a 3 × 3 grid of units. So you need to calculate using the finished block size you want.

To do so, divide the required finished block size by the number of units in the grid layout. For example, if you want to make a 24" (61 cm) square finished block, dividing by 3 (for a 3 × 3 grid) will give you units that are each an 8" (20.5 cm) finished square.

$$24 \div 3 = 8$$

(The finished block size divided by the grid number = finished square size in each grid)

Tip

Finished block sizes are most easily upsized when they are divisible by the grid number (e.g. 3 in the Simplex Star).

SIXTEEN PATCH

In this next example, the Indian Star block is a 4 × 4 grid.

If you want to make a 24" (61 cm) finished block size, divide the finished size by 4 (for the 4 × 4 grid). You will see that the units you need are each 6" (15 cm) finished squares.

To add seam allowances, increase the dimensions as follows:

Squares: Add ½" (1.3 cm) to the finished size of each square.

Half-Square Triangles: Add ⅞" (2.2 cm) to the finished size of both squares.

Quarter-Square Triangles: Add 1¼" (3.2 cm) to the finished size of each square you plan to cut into 4 pieces.

QUILT GRIDS

Here are some common quilt grid dimensions for your convenience.

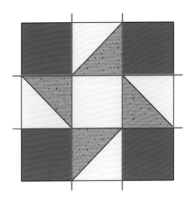

Nine Patch, 3 × 3 grid

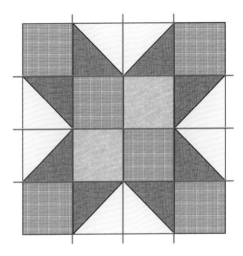

Sixteen Patch, 4 × 4 grid

Four Patch (2 × 2 grid)

Finished Block		
SIZE REQUIRED	FINISHED UNIT SIZE	CUT UNIT SIZE
6" (15 cm)	3" (7.5 cm) square	3.5" (9 cm) square
12" (30.5 cm)	6" (15 cm) square	6.5" (16.5 cm) square
18" (45.5 cm)	9" (23 cm) square	9.5" (24 cm) square
24" (61 cm)	12" (30.5 cm) square	12.5" (31.5 cm) square

Nine Patch (3 × 3 grid)

Finished Block		
SIZE REQUIRED	FINISHED UNIT SIZE	CUT UNIT SIZE
6" (15 cm)	2" (5 cm) square	2.5" (6.5 cm) square
12" (30.5 cm)	4" (10 cm) square	4.5" (11.5 cm) square
18" (45.5 cm)	6" (15 cm) square	6.5" (16.5 cm) square
24" (61 cm)	8" (20.5 cm) square	8.5" (21.5 cm) square

Sixteen Patch (4 × 4 grid)

Finished Block		
SIZE REQUIRED	FINISHED UNIT SIZE	CUT UNIT SIZE
6" (15 cm)	1.5" (3.8 cm) square	2" (5 cm) square
12" (30.5 cm)	3" (7.5 cm) square	3.5" (9 cm) square
18" (45.5 cm)	4.5" (11.5 cm) square	5" (12.5 cm) square
24" (61 cm)	6" (15 cm) square	6.5" (16.5 cm) square

Test Before You Invest

It is always a great idea to create a test block with scrap fabric to make sure you have the exact dimensions you want before cutting up all of your fabric only to find that you made a miscalculation along the way.

Work out the fabric requirements before purchasing or cutting into fabric. This will ensure that you buy enough fabric or can get the required number of pieces out of what you have before you start cutting it. This may save you from making another trip to the store and potential frustration if the fabric you are using is no longer available.

Also, check your measurements and check them again. It never hurt anybody to triple check!

CHAPTER 3

QUILT BLOCKS

Blocks form the basis for quilting patterns and designs. They are frequently combined with other blocks, but can also be used on their own to create a complete quilt using the fabric and orientation of the block to create interest.

Many blocks have traditional meaning or heritage, and as a result many of the quilts we love today use these classic blocks to add life to our designs. In *Quilt Big*, I have explored and supersized some of my favorite blocks, to make quilts, pillows, and runners. A number of the blocks share the same finished size. So if you love the look of a specific block, you can use it in the project as shown (see chapter 4) or swap it with another block to create your own one-of-a-kind patterns.

Additional Blocks

The Scrappy HST Pillow and Home Treasure quilt can also be made into blocks that can be used in other projects if you skip the finishing steps. See the specific projects in chapter 4 for details.

Half-Square Triangle Block

These classic and versatile blocks can be rotated to create countless patterns and styles of quilts. They can also be used to fill space in smaller areas or to create fantastic border designs. The Half-Square Triangle (HST) looks stunning when made with a limited color palette or a large variety of prints.

Finished Block Size: 9" (23 cm) square

Materials
(makes 2 Blocks)

- White fabric, 1 fat quarter (18" × 21" [45.5 cm × 53.5 cm])

- Blue fabric, 1 fat quarter (18" × 21" [45.5 cm × 53.5 cm])

- 12½" (31.5 cm) square ruler

- Erasable fabric marking pen

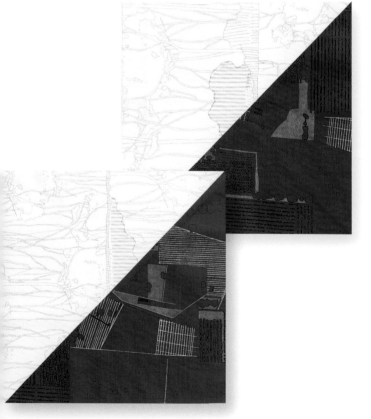

CUTTING INSTRUCTIONS

From the white fabric, cut:

(1) 10" (25.5 cm) square

From the blue fabric, cut:

(1) 10" (25.5 cm) square

All seam allowances are ¼" (6 mm) unless otherwise indicated.

1. Using an erasable fabric marking pen, draw a diagonal line from corner to corner on the wrong side of (1) 10" (25.5 cm) white square (**Figure 1**).

2. Place a white square and a blue square with right sides together and pin. Sew along both sides of the marked line with a ¼" (6 mm) seam allowance, then rotary cut along the diagonal line (**Figure 2**).

3. Open both squares and press the seam towards the darker fabric (**Figure 3**).

4. Trim both blocks to 9½" (24 cm) square. Makes 2 HSTs.

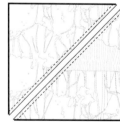

Fig. 1   **Fig. 2**

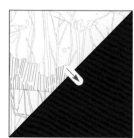

Fig. 3

Lozenge Block

This fun, fast block offers many different layout options. I used a single background fabric, but you could work with lots of low-volume fabrics (light color printed fabric) instead. This is a great block for showcasing large-scale prints or heavily patterned fabrics.

Finished size: 24" (61 cm) square

Materials per block

- Yellow fabric, ¾ yard (0.7 m)
- Gray background fabric, ⅜ yard (34.5 cm)
- 12½" (31.5 cm) square ruler
- Erasable fabric marking pen

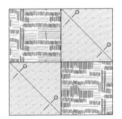

Fig. 1

Fig. 2

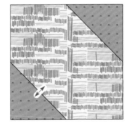

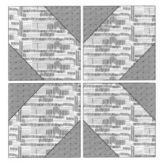

Fig. 3

CUTTING INSTRUCTIONS

From the yellow fabric, cut:
(4) 12½" (31.5 cm) squares

From the grey background fabric, cut:
(8) 6½" (16.5 cm) squares

1. Using an erasable fabric marking pen, draw a diagonal line from corner to corner on the wrong side of (2) 6½" (16.5 cm) grey background squares.

2. Pin the first grey background square to the top right corner of the 12½" (31.5 cm) yellow square with the diagonal running left to right, and pin the second grey background square to the bottom left hand corner with the diagonal running left to right (**Figure 1**).

3. Sew along the diagonal lines. Trim the excess corner fabric, leaving a ¼" (6mm) seam allowance on both corners (**Figure 2**). Press the seams open.

4. Repeat steps 1-3 to make 4 units total.

5. Referring to **Figure 3**, arrange the units as shown, making sure to orient them in the correct direction. Pin and sew the top and bottom rows together, pressing seams open. Then pin and sew the top and bottom row together to complete the L ozenge block, pressing rows open.

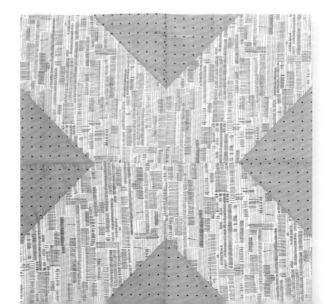

Flying Geese Block

Flying Geese blocks depict geese flying (the large triangles) through the sky (smaller triangles). This block appeals to many for its simplicity and versatility. It can be used on its own or together in groups to make new designs, which is when it really shows distinction. Flying Geese blocks also work well for borders.

Finished Unit Size: 10" × 20" (25.5 cm × 51 cm)
Finished Block Size: 20" (51 cm) square

Materials per block

- Aqua fabric, ⅓ yard (30.5 cm)

- White background fabric, ⅝ yard (57 cm)

- 6½" × 24" (16.5 cm × 61 cm) ruler

- Erasable fabric marking pen

CUTTING INSTRUCTIONS

From the aqua fabric, cut:

(2) 10¾" × 20¾" (27.5 cm × 52.5 cm) rectangles

From the white background fabric, cut:

(4) 10¾" (27.5 cm) squares

All seam allowances are ¼" (6 mm) unless otherwise indicated.

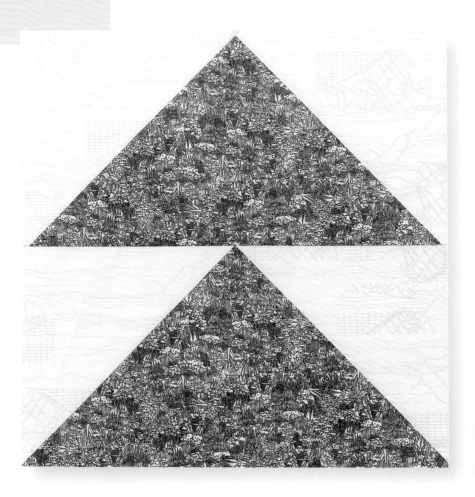

1. Gather (2) 10¾" (27.5 cm) white background squares. Using an erasable fabric marking pen, draw a diagonal line from corner to corner on the wrong side of both squares. Place the first square on the right half of the 10¾" × 20¾" (27.5 cm × 52.5 cm) aqua rectangle (line going from upper left to lower right) with right sides together and edges aligned as shown. Pin the pieces together (**Figure 1**).

2. Sew along the marked diagonal line and trim the excess fabric (**Figure 2**).

3. Press the seam toward the background fabric (**Figure 3**).

4. Repeat steps 1-3 for the second square on the left side of the aqua rectangle. Be sure to orient the white square so the diagonal seams cross at the top center of the rectangle (**Figure 4**).

5. Trim the excess fabric down to ¼" (6 mm) seam allowance so the Flying Geese unit measures 10½" × 20½" (26.5 cm × 52 cm). Make 2 units.

6. Arrange the two Flying Geese units as shown (**Figure 5**).

7. Sew the two units together, pinning and pressing the seam towards the darker fabric.

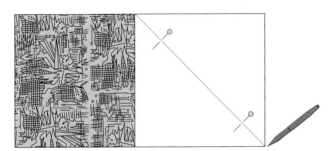

Fig. 1

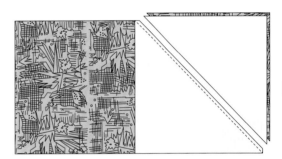

Fig. 2

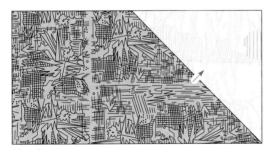

Fig. 3

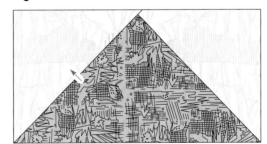

Fig. 4

Fig. 5

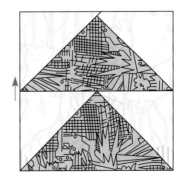

Bow Tie Block

This charming block goes together quickly and is incredibly flexible—simply by changing the orientation of the block you can create a variety of designs. It is also a great block for showcasing fabrics that have characters or mid-scale prints. The following is just one of the many ways that you can turn Bow Tie units into a repeating pattern.

Finished Unit Size: 10" (25.5 cm) square
Finished Block Size: 20" (51 cm) square

Materials per block

- Turquoise fabric, 1 fat eighth
  (9" × 21" [23 cm × 53.5 cm])

- Green fabric, 1 fat eighth
  (9" × 21" [23 cm × 53.5 cm])

- Dark blue fabric, 1 fat eighth
  (9" × 21" [23 cm × 53.5 cm])

- Medium blue fabric, 1 fat eighth
  (9" × 21" [23 cm × 53.5 cm])

- White background fabric, 1 fat quarter
  (18" × 21" [45.5 cm × 53.5 cm])

- Erasable fabric marking pen

CUTTING INSTRUCTIONS

From each of the turquoise, green, dark blue, and medium blue fabrics, cut:

(2) 5½" (14 cm) squares

(2) 3" (7.5 cm) squares

From the white background fabric, cut:

(8) 5½" (14 cm) squares

All seam allowances are ¼" (6 mm) unless otherwise indicated.

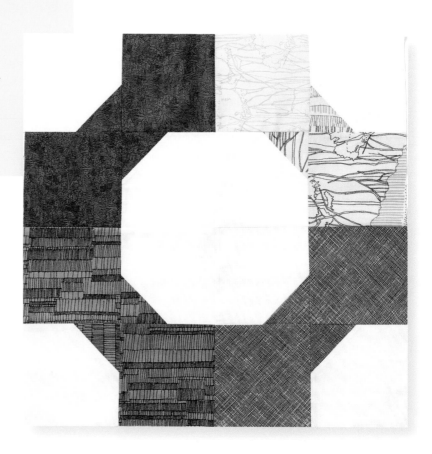

1. Using an erasable fabric marking pen, draw a diagonal line from corner to corner on the wrong side of each 3" (7.5 cm) turquoise square. Place a 3" (7.5 cm) square on the top right-hand corner of a 5½" (14 cm) white background fabric square with right sides together and the diagonal line running from the top left corner to the bottom right corner of the square. Pin in place and sew along this marked line (**Figure 1**). Trim off the corner leaving a ¼" seam allowance (**Figure 2**). Press the seam open (**Figure 3**).

2. In the same manner as step 1, sew together the remaining 3" (7.5 cm) turquoise square and 5½" (14 cm) white background fabric square. You will have 2 corner block squares.

3. Arrange the 5½" (14 cm) turquoise squares and the corner block squares as shown with the corner block squares oriented toward the center (**Figure 4**). Pin and sew the squares together by row. Press the seams toward the turquoise fabric. Pin and sew the rows together to complete a Bow Tie unit. Press the seams toward the turquoise fabric.

4. Repeat steps 1–3 for the remaining green, dark blue, and medium blue fabrics to make 4 Bow Tie units total.

5. Arrange the 4 units as shown (**Figure 5**). Pin and sew the units in each row together. Press the seams in opposite directions.

6. Sew the two rows together to complete the 20½" (52 cm) Bow Tie block.

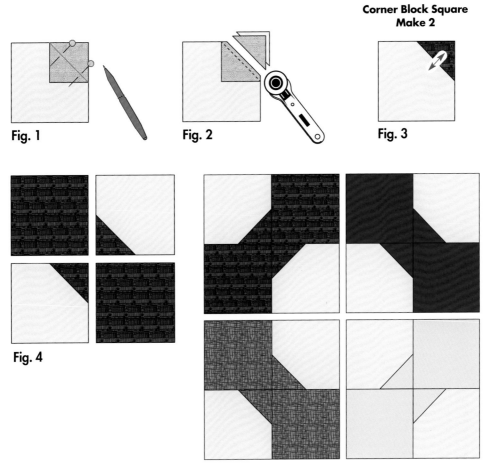

Fig. 1

Fig. 2

Corner Block Square Make 2

Fig. 3

Fig. 4

Fig. 5

Simplex Star Block

This striking block is quick to piece and draws attention from its simple design. You can use a variety of color combinations to change the look of the block.

Finished size: 24" (61 cm) square

Materials per block

- Dark green fabric, ¼ yard (23 cm)

- Light green fabric, 1 fat quarter (18" × 21" [45.5 cm × 53.5 cm])

- White fabric, ⅓ yard (30.5 cm)

- Rotary cutter and self-healing mat

- 12½" (31.5 cm) square ruler

- Erasable fabric marking pen

CUTTING INSTRUCTIONS

From the dark green fabric, cut:

(4) 8½" (21.5 cm) squares

From the light green fabric, cut:

(2) 9" (23 cm) squares

From the white fabric, cut:

(2) 9" (23 cm) squares

(1) 8½" (21.5 cm) square

All seam allowances are ¼" (6 mm) unless otherwise noted.

1. With the erasable fabric marking pen and ruler, draw a diagonal line from corner to corner on the wrong side of (1) 9" (23 cm) white square. Place the white square on top of a light green square with right sides together and pin in place. Sew along either side of the marked line with a ¼" (6 mm) seam allowance, then rotary cut along the diagonal line (**Figure 1**).

2. Open both squares and press the seams towards the darker fabric. This makes 2 Half-Square Triangles (refer to the Half-Square Triangle Block directions in this chapter for tips). Trim the HSTs to 8½" (21.5 cm) square (**Figure 2**).

3. Repeat steps 1–2 with the remaining white and light green squares. Make 4 HST blocks total.

4. Arrange the (4) 8½" (21.5 cm) dark green squares, the (4) 8½" (21.5 cm) HST blocks, and the (1) 8½" (21.5 cm) white square as shown, making sure the light green triangles are oriented in the correct direction (**Figure 3**).

5. Pin and sew the blocks together by row. Press seams towards the dark green blocks in the first and third rows and toward the light green in the second row. Sew each of the rows together to complete the block, pinning and pressing seams toward the dark green fabric (**Figure 4**).

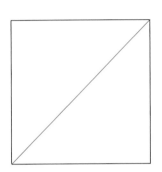

Fig. 1

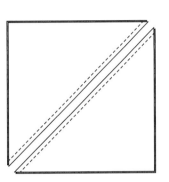

Fig. 2   **Half-Square Triangle Unit**
Make 4

8½" (21.5 cm)

8½" (21.5 cm)

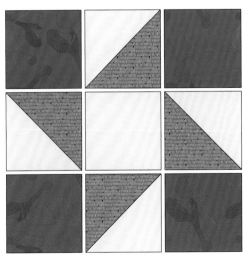

Fig. 3

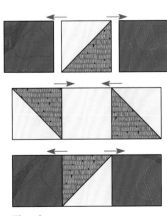

Fig. 4

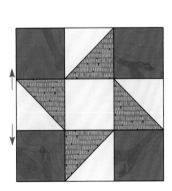

Log Cabin Block

Log Cabins are a great first block for beginners. If you're a new quilter, this variation on the classic design will help boost your confidence to try a new technique. For more experienced quilters, making this design will grow your skills by showcasing this block in a fresh way.

Finished Block Size: 24½" (62 cm)

Materials per block

- Yellow fabric, 1 fat quarter (18" × 21" [45.5 cm × 53.5 cm])

- White and orange fabric, ⅙ yard (15.5 cm)

- Mustard fabric, ⅙ yard (15.5 cm)

- Cream fabric, ⅛ yard (11.5 cm)

- Orange fabric, ¼ yard (23 cm)

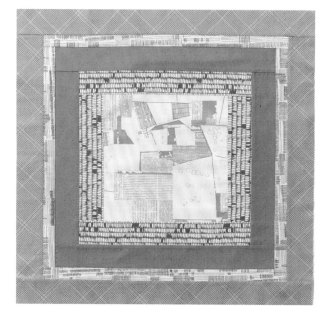

CUTTING INSTRUCTIONS

From the yellow fabric, cut:
(1) 11" (28 cm) square for the center

From the white and orange fabric, cut
(2) 2½" (6.5 cm) strips × WOF (width-of-fabric); subcut into (2) 2½" × 11" (6.5 cm × 28 cm) strips and (2) 2½" × 15" (6.5 cm × 38 cm) strips

From the mustard fabric, cut
(2) 2½" (6.5 cm) strips × WOF; subcut into (2) 2½" × 15" (6.5 cm × 38 cm) strips and (2) 2½" × 19" (6.5 cm × 48.5 cm) strips

From the cream fabric, cut
(2) 1½" (3.8 cm) strips × WOF; subcut into (2) 1½" × 19" (3.8 cm × 48.5 cm) strips and (2) 1½" × 21" (3.8 cm × 53.5 cm) strips

From the orange fabric, cut
(3) 2½" (6.5 cm) strips × WOF; subcut into (2) 2½" × 21" (6.5 cm × 53.5 cm) strips and (2) 2½" × 25" (6.5 cm × 63.5 cm) strips

All seams are ¼" (6 mm) unless otherwise noted.

Tips

PRESSING:

Be sure to set your seams when pressing to ensure straight lines in your blocks (see chapter 1 for more pressing tips).

PINNING:

Before you sew a strip to the Log Cabin block, fold the strip in half (so that the short ends meet) and finger press a mark at the center length, then fold the side of the block you will be sewing the strip to in half and finger press a mark. Before you pin the strip to the block, line up and pin the marks, and pin the edges of the strip. This will ensure that the strip is evenly distributed along your block, so it will sit nice and flat and not stretch out as your block grows.

1. Arrange the yellow center square face-up with (1) 2½" × 11" (6.5 × 28 cm) white and orange strip on either side. Pin the strips to the block with right sides together and sew to either side of the square (**Figure 1**). Press the seams outward.

2. Pin and sew the 2½" × 15" (6.5 cm × 38 cm) white and orange strips to the top and bottom of the center yellow square. Press the seams outward (**Figure 2**). The block now measures 15" (38 cm) square.

3. Following steps 1 and 2, sew the second round of the block using the (2) 2½" × 15" (6.5 cm × 38 cm) mustard strips for the sides and (2) 2½" × 19" (6.5 cm × 48.5 cm) mustard strips for the top and bottom. Press the seams outward. Your block now measures 19" (48.5 cm) square (**Figure 3**).

4. Sew the third round of the block using the (2) 1½" × 19" (3.8 cm × 48.5 cm) cream strips on the sides of the block and (2) 1½" × 21" (3.8 cm × 53.5 cm) cream strips on the top and bottom. Press seams outward. Your block now measures 21" (53.5 cm) square.

5. Sew the fourth round of the block using the (2) 2½" × 21" (6.5 cm × 53.5 cm) orange strips on the sides of the block and the (2) 2½" × 25" (6.5 cm × 63.5 cm) orange strips on the top and bottom. Press the seams outwards. The block should measure 25" (63.5 cm) square (**Figure 4**).

Fig. 1

Fig. 2

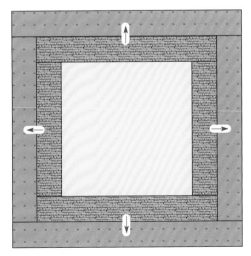

Fig. 3

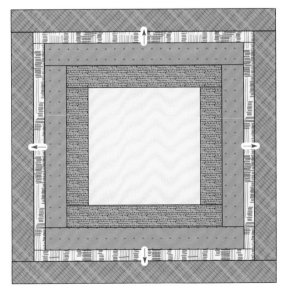

Fig. 4

Churn Dash Block

This traditional geometric quilt block has been beloved for generations and still has great relevance in quilting today. You can easily change the look of this block by using a variety of fabrics or by showcasing a featured fabric in the center square.

Finished Block Size: 24" (61 cm) square

Materials per block

- Turquoise fabric, ⅓ yard (30.5 cm)
- White background fabric, ½ yard (45.5 cm)
- 12½" (31.5 cm) square ruler
- Erasable fabric marking pen

CUTTING INSTRUCTIONS

From the turquoise fabric, cut

(2) 9" (23 cm) squares

(4) 4½" × 8½" (11.5 cm × 21.5 cm) rectangles

From the white background fabric, cut:

(2) 9" (23 cm) squares

(1) 8½" (21.5 cm) square

(4) 4½" × 8½" (11.5 cm × 21.5 cm) rectangles

All seam allowances are ¼" (6 mm) unless otherwise indicated.

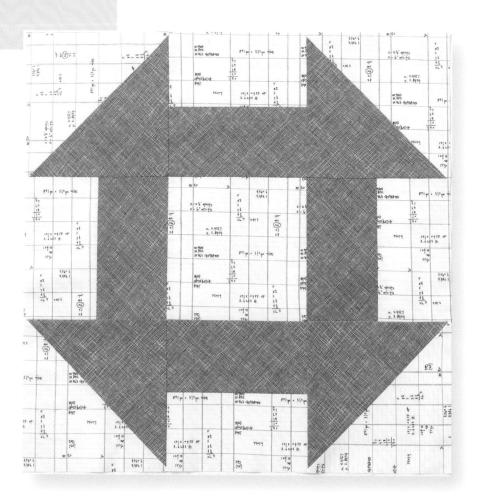

1. Draw a diagonal line from corner to corner on the wrong side of a 9" (23 cm) white background fabric square. Pin the white square onto a 9" (23 cm) turquoise square, right sides together and edges aligned. Sew along both sides of the marked line with a ¼" (6 mm) seam allowance. Rotary cut along the diagonal line (**Figure 1**). Open both squares and press the seams toward the darker fabric. Trim the Half-Square Triangles (HSTs) to 8½" (21.5 cm) square (**Figure 2**).

2. Repeat step 1 with the remaining 9" (23 cm) white background fabric square and 9" (23 cm) turquoise square. Make 4 HSTs total.

3. Set (1) 4½" × 8½" (11.5 cm × 21.5 cm) white rectangle and (1) 4½" × 8½" (11.5 cm × 21.5 cm) turquoise rectangle with right sides together and pin along one long edge.

Sew with a ¼" (6 mm) seam allowance (**Figure 3**). Press the seam toward the turquoise fabric. Repeat with the remaining rectangles. Make 4 rectangle pairs total.

4. Arrange the HSTs and rectangle pairs as shown (**Figure 4**), making sure all of the turquoise fabric pieces are oriented toward the 8½" (21.5 cm) square white background fabric center.

5. Pin and sew the finished pieces together by rows, pressing the seams toward the turquoise fabric in each row.

6. Pin and sew the rows together to complete the block, pressing the seams toward the turquoise fabric.

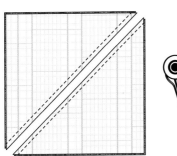

Fig. 1

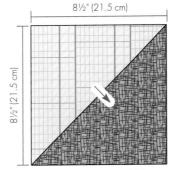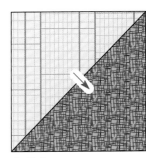

Fig. 2

Half-Square Triangle Unit
Make 4

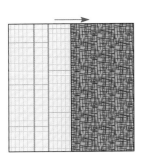

Fig. 3

Rectangle Pairs
Make 4

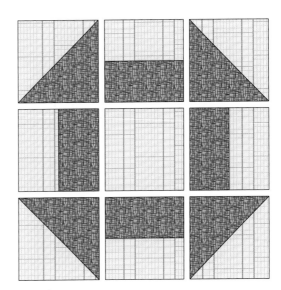

Fig. 4

Mosaic Block

When a block is set diagonally, it is said to be "on point." While on-point blocks may look tricky at first, when you break them down it is simple to achieve this distinctive look for your blocks. With its geometric look, the Mosaic block showcases how traditional blocks can still look modern and on trend.

Finished Block Size: 18" (45.5 cm) square

Materials per block

- Dark green fabric, 1 fat quarter (18" × 21" [45.5 cm × 53.5 cm])

- Light green fabric, 1 fat quarter (18" × 21" [45.5 cm × 53.5 cm])

- Rotary cutter and self-healing mat

- Erasable fabric marking pen

CUTTING INSTRUCTIONS

From the dark green fabric, cut:

(2) 3¾" × 7" (9.5 cm × 18 cm) rectangles

(2) 3¾" × 13½" (9.5 cm × 34.5 cm) rectangles

(2) 5½" (14 cm) squares

From the light green fabric, cut:

(1) 7" (18 cm) square

(2) 5½" (14 cm) squares

(6) 5⅜" (13.5 cm) squares; subcut on the diagonal once

All seam allowances are ¼" (6 mm) unless otherwise noted.

1. Pin (1) 3¾" × 7" (9.5 cm × 18 cm) dark green rectangle to either side of the 7" (18 cm) light green square with right sides together and sew. Press seams outwards. Pin and sew (1) 3¾" × 13½" (9.5 cm × 34.5 cm) dark green rectangle to the top of this block and the other to the bottom (**Figure 1**). Press seams toward the dark green fabric.

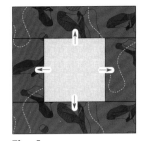

Fig. 1

Fig. 2

2. Following the Half-Square Triangle (HST) block directions in this chapter, make 4 HSTs using the (2) 5½" (14 cm) dark green squares and (2) 5½" (14 cm) light green squares (**Figure 2**). Trim the HSTs to 5" (12.5 cm) square.

5" (12.5 cm)

5" (12.5 cm)

Half-Square Triangle Unit
Make 4

3. Pin (1) 5⅜" (13.5 cm) triangle along the right side of one of the HSTs from step 2. Sew in place as shown and press seam outward (**Figure 3**). There will be a ¼" (6 mm) tip running past the block at the bottom. Press seam outwards.

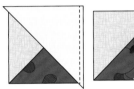
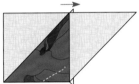

Fig. 3

4. Referring to **Figure 4**, pin a second 5⅜" (13.5 cm) triangle along the bottom dark green side of the HST as shown. Sew and press seam outward. Trim tips from the center of the long diagonal side to complete the side-setting triangle unit.

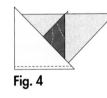
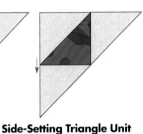

Fig. 4

Side-Setting Triangle Unit
Make 4

5. Following steps 3–4, make 4 side-setting triangle units total.

6. Mark a center crease in one side of the center square that has a shorter dark green rectangle, then mark a center crease in the long side of the side-setting triangle unit. Line up the center crease along the dark green rectangle with the center crease from the side-setting triangle unit (this should fall at the pointed end of the dark green triangle), and pin in place as shown (**Figure 5**). Sew and press the seams towards the dark green rectangles. Repeat this step on the opposite side with a second side-setting triangle (**Figure 6**).

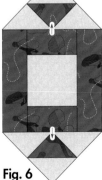

Fig. 5

Fig. 6

7. In the same manner as step 6, pin and sew the remaining side-setting triangle units to the center square (**Figure 7**).

Fig. 7

Lola Block

This block may be simple to construct, but placing it "on point" takes your skills to the next level. Whether you use heavily printed fabrics or bold solids, the colors and prints you choose will allow this block to shine.

Finished size: 28" (71 cm) square

Materials per block

- Teal fabric, 1 fat quarter (18" × 21" [45.5 cm × 53.5 cm])

- Mustard fabric, 1 fat quarter (18" × 21" [45.5 cm × 53.5 cm])

- Cream fabric, ⅓ yard (30.5 cm)

- Background fabric, ½ yard (45.5 cm)

- Rotary cutter and self-healing mat

CUTTING INSTRUCTIONS

From the teal fabric, cut:
(4) 5½" (14 cm) squares

From the mustard fabric, cut:
(4) 5½" (14 cm) squares

From the cream fabric, cut:
(4) 5½" × 10½" (14 cm × 26.5 cm) rectangles

From the background fabric, cut:
(2) 15⅛" (38.5 cm) squares; subcut diagonally once

All seam allowances are ¼" (6 mm) unless otherwise noted.

1. Arrange (2) 5½" (14 cm) teal squares and (2) 5½" (14 cm) mustard squares in a Four Patch formation. Pin the squares in each row with right sides together and sew, pressing the seam towards the teal fabric.

2. Sew the top and bottom rows together, pressing the seam open (**Figure 1**).

3. Arrange the Four Patch unit, the remaining 5½" (14 cm) teal and mustard squares, and the (4) 5½" × 10½" (14 cm × 26.5 cm) cream rectangles as shown (**Figure 2**).

4. Pin and sew the blocks together with right sides facing by row, pressing seams towards the darker fabrics. Pin and sew the rows together, taking your time to match up the seams. Press the seams open.

5. Gently fold the block to mark a center crease on one side. Then fold one of the background triangles in half to mark a center crease along the diagonal. Placing right sides together, match up the center creases of the block and triangle, then pin in place (**Figure 3**). Your triangle will extend past the Lola block (this creates the seam allowance in the next step). Sew this seam and press the seam outward. Repeat on the opposite side with another background triangle (**Figure 4**).

6. Repeat step 5 with the two remaining background triangles. Trim the block to 28½" (72.5 cm) square, making sure you have a ¼" (6 mm) seam allowance at the intersecting points (**Figure 5**).

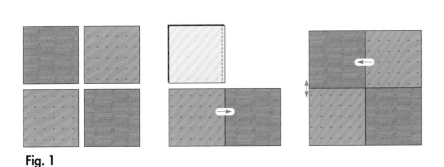

Fig. 1

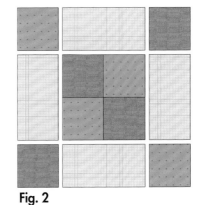

Fig. 2

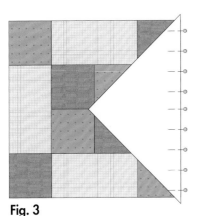

Fig. 3

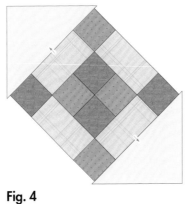

Fig. 4

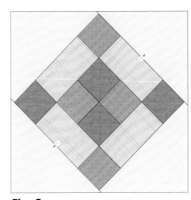

Fig. 5

Strip Heart Block

I have always loved heart-shaped blocks. I think they speak to the very essence of what quilting is about. They are a great design to show someone how much you care and can make sweet quilts to gift for Valentine's Day. This Strip Heart block certainly attests to this. Its sleek, modern design makes it a perfect gift for that special someone in your life. As a bonus, the size of the blocks featured here allow you to use prints that showcase lots of detail.

Finished Block Size: 18" (45.5 cm) square

Materials per block

- Dark orange fabric, 1 fat quarter
  (18" × 21" [45.5 cm × 53.5 cm])

- Light orange fabric, 1 fat eighth
  (9" × 21" [23 cm × 53.5 cm])

- Peach fabric, 1 fat eighth
  (9" × 21" [23 cm × 53.5 cm])

- Cream background fabric, 1 fat quarter
  (18" × 21" [45.5 cm × 53.5 cm])

- 12½" (31.5 cm) square ruler

- Erasable fabric marking pen

CUTTING INSTRUCTIONS

From the dark orange fabric, cut:
(1) 9¾" × 18¾" (25 cm × 47.5 cm) rectangle

(2) 5¼" × 9¾" (13.5 cm × 25 cm) rectangles

From the light orange fabric, cut:
(1) 2¾" × 18½" (7 cm × 47 cm) strip

From the peach fabric, cut:
(1) 2¾" × 18½" (7 cm × 47 cm) strip

From the cream background fabric, cut:
(2) 9¾" (25 cm) squares

(4) 5¼" (13.5 cm) squares

All seam allowances are ¼" (6 mm) unless otherwise noted.

1. Using an erasable fabric marking pen, draw a diagonal line from corner to corner on the wrong side of (2) 9¾" (25 cm) cream squares. Place the first square on the right half of the 9¾" × 18¾" (25 cm × 47.5 cm) dark orange rectangle (line going from upper left to lower right) with right sides together and edges aligned as shown. Pin the pieces together and sew along the marked diagonal line. Trim the excess fabric as shown, leaving a ¼" (6 mm) seam allowance (**Figure 1**). Press the seam toward the cream fabric.

2. In the same manner as step 1, sew the second square on the left side of the Flying Geese unit. Be sure to orient the square so the diagonal seams cross at the top center of the block (**Figure 2**). Trim the seam allowance to ¼" (6 mm). The block should measure 9½" × 18½" (24 cm × 47 cm).

3. In the same way as steps 1 and 2, make 2 Flying Geese units with the (4) 5¼" (13.5 cm) cream squares and (2) 5¼" × 9¾" (13.5 cm × 25 cm) dark orange rectangles, trimming each unit to 5" × 9½" (12.5 cm × 24 cm). Sew these two smaller Flying Geese units together on one short side (**Figure 3**).

4. Pin and sew the 2¾" × 18½" (7 cm × 47 cm) light orange and peach strips with right sides together along the longer length. Press the seam open (**Figure 4**).

5. Referring to **Figure 5**, arrange the pieces as shown. Pin and sew the pieces together along the long edges. Press the seams toward the center unit.

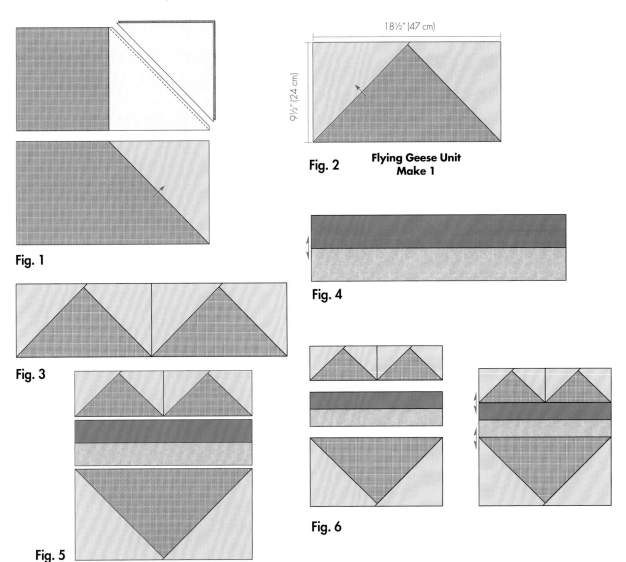

Fig. 1

Fig. 2   **Flying Geese Unit
Make 1**

18½" (47 cm)

9½" (24 cm)

Fig. 3

Fig. 4

Fig. 5

Fig. 6

Millennium Block

Bold and versatile, this block can be made with lots of fabrics as shown or with a limited color palette and heavily patterned fabrics for a completely different look. You could even fussy cut your fabric to make a statement in the center square.

Finished Block Size: 30" (76 cm) square

Materials per block

- Gold 1 fabric (shown as blue and yellow geometric), ⅓ yard (30.5 cm)

- Gold 2 fabric (shown as light yellow), ¼ yard (23 cm)

- Gold 3 fabric (shown as light beige grid), ¼ yard (23 cm)

- Gold 4 fabric (shown as dark gold), 1 fat quarter (18" x 21" [45.5 cm x 53.5 cm])

- Gold 5 fabric (shown as black and yellow print), ½ yard (45.5 cm)

CUTTING INSTRUCTIONS

From gold 1 fabric, cut:
(1) 10½" (26.5 cm) square

(4) 5½" (14 cm) squares

From gold 2 fabric, cut:
(4) 3" × 10½" (7.5 cm × 26.5 cm) rectangles

From gold 3 fabric, cut:
(4) 3" × 10½" (7.5 cm × 26.5 cm) rectangles

From gold 4 fabric, cut:
(8) 5¾" (14.5 cm) squares

From gold 5 fabric, cut:
(4) 5¾" × 10¾" (14.5 cm × 27.5 cm) rectangles

(4) 5½" (14 cm) squares

(4) 5½" × 10½" (14 cm × 26.5 cm) rectangles

All seam allowances are ¼" (6 mm) unless otherwise noted.

1. Pin (1) 3" × 10½" (7.5 cm × 26.5 cm) gold 2 rectangle and (1) 3" × 10½" (7.5 cm × 26.5 cm) gold 3 rectangle together along the long edge with right sides facing and sew (**Figure 1**). Press the seams open. Make 4 pairs.

2. Pin (1) 5½" (14 cm) gold 1 square and (1) 5½" (14 cm) gold 5 square with right sides together and sew along one edge. Press the seams open. Make 4 pairs. Referring to **Figure 2**, pin and sew (1) 5½" × 10½" (14 cm × 26.5 cm) gold 5 rectangle to the top of each pair as shown to make 4 corner units.

3. Following the Flying Geese directions in this chapter, make 4 Flying Geese units using the (8) 5¾" (14.5 cm) gold 4 squares and the (4) 5¾" × 10¾" (14.5 cm × 27.5 cm) gold 5 rectangles. Trim the Flying Geese units to 5½" × 10½" (14 cm × 26.5 cm) (**Figure 3**).

4. Arrange the rectangle pairs from step 1 with the Flying Geese units, so the point of each Flying Geese unit is against the long side of the gold 3 rectangle. Pin the pieces along the long edge with right sides together and sew. Press the seam toward the Flying Geese (**Figure 4**). Make 4 units total.

5. Arrange the finished pieces around the 10½" (26.5 cm) gold 1 square as shown (**Figure 5**).

6. Pin and sew the units together by row, making sure the seams align. Press the seams open.

7. Pin and sew the rows together, pressing seams open.

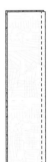

Fig. 1

Rectangle Pair
Make 4

Fig. 2

Corner Unit
Make 4

Fig. 3   **Flying Geese Unit**
Make 4

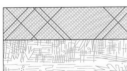

Fig. 4

Make 4

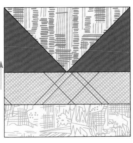

Fig. 5

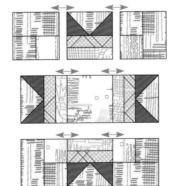
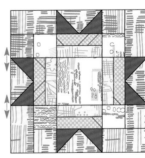

Ohio Star Block

Made up of a Nine Patch block containing Quarter-Square Triangles and squares, this block looks different depending on the placement of the background color and prints.
The Ohio Star is all about getting those points neatly lined up for a sharp finish.

Finished Block Size: 15" (38 cm) square

Materials per block

- Orange fabrics, (5) fat sixteenths
  (each 9" × 10½" [23 cm × 26.5 cm])

- White/gray spot background fabric,
  1 fat quarter (18" × 21" [45.5 cm × 53.5 cm])

- Rotary cutter and self-healing mat

- Erasable fabric marking pen

CUTTING INSTRUCTIONS

From each of 4 orange fabrics, cut:
(1) 4½" (11.5 cm) square (for a total of 4 orange squares)

From 1 orange fabric, cut:
(1) 5½" (14 cm) center square

From the white/gray spot background fabric, cut:
(4) 4½" (11.5 cm) squares

(4) 5½" (14 cm) squares

All seam allowances are ¼" (6 mm) unless otherwise noted.

1. With a rotary cutter, cut (4) 4½ (11.5 cm) orange fabric squares and (4) 4½ (11.5 cm) white/gray spot background fabric squares in half once on the diagonal.

2. Sew 2 background fabric triangles and 2 orange triangles (from the same fabric) together in pairs along one short bias side. Press the seams towards the orange fabric (**Figure 1**).

3. Arrange two triangles from step 1 right-side up with the orange triangles opposite each other. Place the triangles right sides together, then pin and sew along the diagonal. Press the seam open and trim the Quarter-Square Triangle to 5½" (14 cm) square (**Figure 2**).

4. Repeat steps 1–3 to make 4 Quarter-Square Triangles total.

5. Referring to **Figure 3**, arrange the 4 Quarter-Square Triangles, (4) 5½" (14 cm) background fabric squares and 5½" (14 cm) orange center square as shown. Pin and sew the finished pieces together in each row, making sure the seams align. Press the seams open. Pin and sew all 3 rows together. Press the seams open.

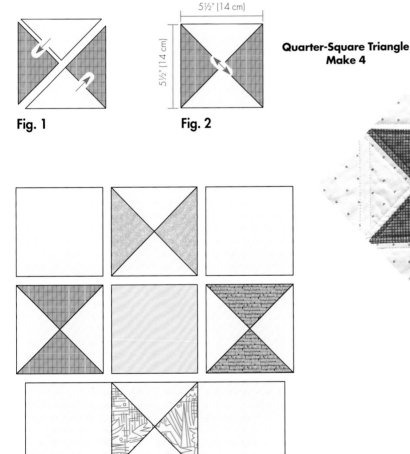

5½" (14 cm)

5½" (14 cm)

Quarter-Square Triangle
Make 4

Fig. 1

Fig. 2

Fig. 3

Rising Star Block

I love this star block. No matter which type of print or pattern you choose—florals, novelty, plain, or geometric—you always end up with a beautiful result.

Finished Block Size: 20" (51 cm) square

Materials per block

- Blue 1 fabric (shown as blue/orange),
  1 fat quarter (18" × 21" [45.5 cm × 53.5 cm])

- Blue 2 fabric (shown as dark blue grid),
  1 fat eighth (9" × 21" [23 cm × 53.5 cm])

- Blue 3 fabric (shown as mid blue/black),
  1 fat quarter (18" × 21" [45.5 cm × 53.5 cm])

- Blue 4 fabric (shown as white and blue stripe),
  ⅓ yard (30.5 cm)

- Erasable fabric marking pen

CUTTING INSTRUCTIONS

To keep the fabrics organized, use an erasable fabric marking pen to label the back of each piece with the number.

From blue 1 fabric, cut:

(1) 5½" (14 cm) square

(4) 3¼" × 5¾" (8.5 cm × 14.5 cm) rectangles

(4) 3" (7.5 cm) squares

From blue 2 fabric, cut:

(8) 3¼" (8.5 cm) squares

From blue 3 fabric, cut:

(8) 5¾" (14.5 cm) squares

From blue 4 fabric, cut:

(4) 5¾" × 10¾" (14.5 cm × 27.5 cm) rectangles

(4) 5 ½" (14 cm) squares

All seam allowances are ¼" (6 mm) unless otherwise indicated.

1. Following the Flying Geese directions in this chapter, make 4 Flying Geese units with the (8) 3¼" (8.5 cm) blue 2 squares and the (4) 3¼" × 5¾" (8.5 cm × 14.5 cm) blue 1 rectangles. Trim the Flying Geese to 3" × 5½" (7.5 cm × 14 cm) (**Figure 1**).

2. Arrange the 4 Flying Geese, the 5½" (14 cm) blue 1 square, and the (4) 3" (7.5 cm) squares as shown (**Figure 2**).

3. Pin and sew the finished pieces together in each row, making sure the seams align. Press the seams open (**Figure 3**).

4. Sew the rows together, pinning and pressing seams open.

5. Following the Flying Geese directions, make 4 Flying Geese units with the (8) 5¾" (14.5 cm) blue 3 squares and the (4) 5¾" × 10¾" (14.5 cm × 27.5 cm) blue 4 rectangles. Trim the Flying Geese to 5½" × 10½" (14 cm × 26.5 cm).

6. In the same manner as steps 3–4, arrange the Flying Geese units and (4) 5½" (14 cm) blue 4 squares around the finished center block. Pin and sew the finished pieces together with right sides facing, pressing the seams open (**Figure 4**).

**Flying Geese Unit
Make 4**

Fig. 1

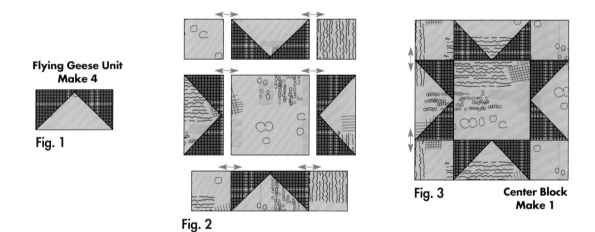

Fig. 2

Fig. 3   **Center Block
Make 1**

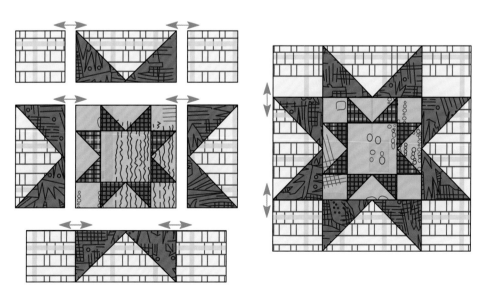

Fig. 4

Sarah's Choice Block

Whether you make this block scrappy, two-toned, in rainbow hues, or ombré, the end result is always eye-catching and appealing to any audience. With its stunning Pinwheel block center, this block is quick to make and open to endless color combinations.

Finished Block Size: 24" (61 cm) square

Materials per block

- Purple 1 fabric, 1 fat quarter
  (18" × 21" [45.5 cm × 53.5 cm])

- Purple 2 fabric, 1 fat quarter
  (18" × 21" [45.5 cm × 53.5 cm])

- White/gray spot background fabric,
  ⅜ yard (34.5 cm)

- 12½" (31.5 cm) square ruler

- 6½" (16.5 cm) Bloc Loc Half-Square Triangle
  Square Up Ruler (optional)

- 6" × 12" (15 cm × 30.5 cm) Bloc Loc Flying
  Geese Square Up Ruler (optional)

- Erasable fabric marking pen

CUTTING INSTRUCTIONS

To keep the fabrics organized, use the erasable fabric marking pen to label the back of each piece with the number.

From purple 1 fabric, cut:
(2) 7" (18 cm) squares

(4) 6¾" (17 cm) squares

From purple 2 fabric, cut:
(2) 7" (18 cm) squares

(4) 6¾" (17 cm) squares

From the white/gray spot background fabric, cut:
(4) 6¾" × 12¾" (17 cm × 32.5 cm) rectangles

(4) 6½" (16.5 cm) squares

All seam allowances are ¼" (6 mm) unless otherwise indicated.

1. Using the 7" (18 cm) purple 1 and purple 2 squares and following the Half-Square Triangle directions in this chapter, make 4 Half-Square Triangles (HSTs). Trim the HSTs to 6½" (16.5 cm) square (**Figure 1**).

2. Referring to **Figure 2**, arrange the 4 purple HSTs in 2 rows of 2 to form a Pinwheel block. Pin the finished pieces in each row with right sides together and sew. Sew the rows together.

3. Referring to the directions for Flying Geese in this chapter, make 4 Flying Geese units using the 6¾" (17 cm) purple 1 and purple 2 squares and the 6¾" × 12¾" (17 cm × 32.5 cm) background fabric rectangles.

(Each side will be a different purple, so be sure to sew the same fabric to the same side each time.) Trim the Flying Geese units to 6½" × 12½" (16.5 cm × 31.5 cm) (**Figure 3**).

4. Arrange the finished pieces and 6½" (16.5 cm) background fabric squares as shown (**Figure 4**).

5. Pin and sew the finished pieces and squares together by row, making sure your seams align. Press seams open.

6. Pin and sew the rows together, pressing seams open.

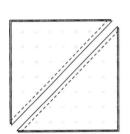

Fig. 1

6½" (16.5 cm)

6½" (16.5 cm)

Half-Square Triangle Unit
Make 4

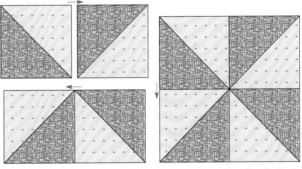

Fig. 2

Pinwheel Block
Make 1

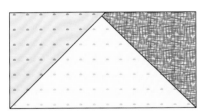

Fig. 3

Flying Geese Unit
Make 4

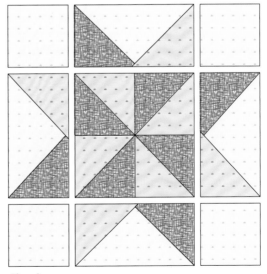

Fig. 4

Missouri Star Block

While the origins of this design date back to the American Civil War, the Missouri Star looks as modern today as it did then. It is often used in sampler quilts, but works just as well on its own as a repeated block. It is easy to see why this block has remained popular for generations.

Finished Block Size: 20" (51 cm) square

Materials per block

- Green 1 fabric (shown as light teal),
  1 fat eighth (9" × 21" [23 cm × 53.5 cm])

- Green 2 fabric (shown as dark teal),
  1 fat eighth (9" × 21" [23 cm × 53.5 cm])

- Green 3 fabric (shown as medium teal),
  ⅜ yard (34.5 cm)

- White/gray spot background fabric,
  1 fat quarter (18" × 21"
  [45.5 cm × 53.5 cm])

- Rotary cutter and self-healing mat

- 12½" (31.5 cm) square ruler

- Erasable fabric marking pen

CUTTING INSTRUCTIONS

To keep the fabrics organized, use the erasable fabric marking pen to label the back of each piece with the number.

From green 1 fabric, cut:
(2) 6" (15 cm) squares; subcut diagonally once

From green 2 fabric, cut:
(2) 6¼" (16 cm) squares; subcut diagonally twice

From green 3 fabric, cut:
(4) 5½" (14 cm) squares

(1) 11¼" (28.5 cm) square; subcut diagonally twice

From the white/gray spot background fabric, cut:
(1) 7⅝" (19.5 cm) square

(2) 6¼" (16 cm) squares; subcut diagonally twice

All seam allowances are ¼" (6 mm) unless otherwise indicated.

1. Fold the (4) 6" (15 cm) green 1 triangles in half to make a center crease along the longest side, being careful not to stretch the long bias edge. Fold the 7⅝" (19.5 cm) background fabric square in half in both directions to make a center crease on each side.

2. Referring to **Figure 1**, place the long edge of a green triangle on one side of the background fabric square with right sides together, matching up the center crease marks with the raw edges; pin in place. (The triangle tips will extend past your square, but you will need this seam allowance shortly.) Sew along this side, pressing the seam towards the green fabric. Repeat on the opposite side of the square with a second green triangle. Repeat for the remaining sides. Trim the tips. The block should measure 10½" (26.5 cm) square (**Figure 2**).

3. Referring to **Figure 3**, arrange the background fabric triangles cut from the 6¼" (16.5 cm) squares and the green 2 triangles cut from the 6¼" (16.5 cm) squares in pairs with

one pair a reverse of the other. Sew them together as shown along one short bias side. Make 4 pairs of each.

4. Fold each 11¼" (28.5 cm) green 3 triangle in half to mark the center. Pin and sew the pairs of triangles from step 3 to each side of the green 3 triangle, lining up the edge on the center crease and pinning the pieces in place (**Figure 4**). Press the seams towards the smaller triangles and trim to 5½" × 10½" (14 cm × 26.5 cm) rectangle units.

5. Arrange the center square, rectangle units, and 5½" (14 cm) green 3 squares as shown (**Figure 5**).

6. Sew the finished pieces together in each row, pinning to make sure your seams align and pressing seams open.

7. Sew the rows together, pinning and pressing seams open.

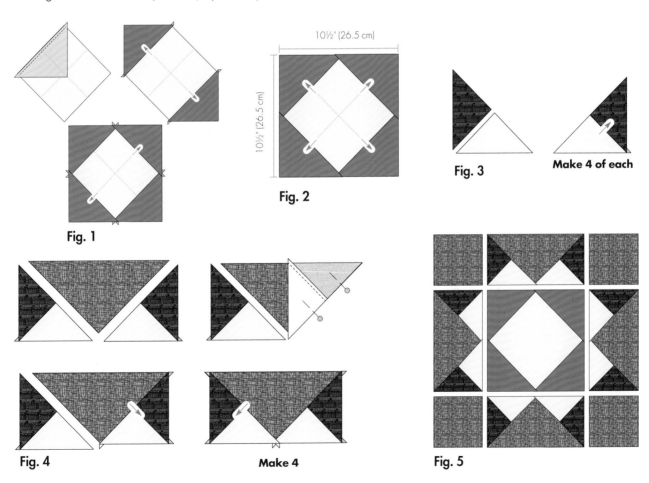

10½" (26.5 cm)

10½" (26.5 cm)

Fig. 1

Fig. 2

Fig. 3

Make 4 of each

Fig. 4

Make 4

Fig. 5

Indian Star Block

Made with Four Patch and Flying Geese units, this simple yet effective design packs a punch. You can use only two fabrics for a simple effect or try four fabrics for a scrappier look.

Finished Block Size: 24" (61 cm) square

Materials per block

- Pink fabric, 1 fat quarter (18" × 21" [45.5 cm × 53.5 cm])

- Orange fabric, ¼ yard (23 cm)

- White/orange fabric, 1 fat eighth (9" × 21" [23 cm × 53.5 cm])

- Gray background fabric, ⅜ yard (34.5 cm)

- Erasable fabric marking pen

CUTTING INSTRUCTIONS

From the pink fabric, cut:
(8) 6¾" (17 cm) squares

From the orange fabric, cut:
(6) 6½" (16.5 cm) squares

From the white/orange fabric, cut:
(2) 6½" (16.5 cm) squares

From the gray background fabric, cut:
(4) 6¾" × 12¾" (17 cm × 32.5 cm) rectangles

All seam allowances are ¼" (6 mm) unless otherwise indicated.

Mix and Match

This block is featured in the Indian Star Mini Quilt in chapter 4, but its 24" (61 cm) size means you can easily use it in place of or with the existing blocks in the Lozenge Quilt and the Simplex Star Quilt, both in chapter 4.

1. Gather (2) 6¾" (17 cm) pink squares. Using an erasable fabric marking pen, draw a diagonal line from corner to corner on the wrong side of each square. Place the first square on the right half of the 6¾" × 12¾" (17 cm × 32.5 cm) gray background fabric rectangle (line going from upper left to lower right) with right sides together and edges aligned. Pin the pieces together. Sew along the marked diagonal line. Trim the excess fabric as shown, leaving a ¼" (6 mm) seam allowance (**Figure 1**). Press the seam toward the background fabric.

2. Repeat step 1 for the second square on the left side of the Flying Geese unit, orienting the square so the diagonal seams cross at the top center of the rectangle.

3. Trim the excess fabric from the Flying Geese unit down to ¼" (6 mm) seam allowance so that it measures 6½" × 12½" (16.5 cm × 31.5 cm) (**Figure 2**). Make 4 Flying Geese units.

4. Referring to **Figure 3**, arrange (2) 6½" (16.5 cm) orange fabric squares and (2) 6½" (16.5 cm) white/orange fabric squares in a Four Patch unit. Pin and sew the squares together by row, pressing toward the darker fabric. Then sew the two rows together.

5. Arrange the Four Patch unit, 4 Flying Geese units, and (4) 6½" (16.5 cm) orange fabric squares as shown in **Figure 4**.

6. Sew the 6½" (16.5 cm) square to either side of the Flying Geese units in the first and third rows, pinning and pressing the seams towards the orange fabric. Sew the Flying Geese units to the center Four Patch unit, pressing the seams open.

7. Sew the rows together to complete the block, pinning and pressing rows open.

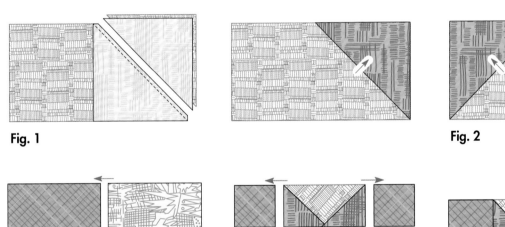

Fig. 1

Fig. 2

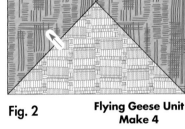

**Flying Geese Unit
Make 4**

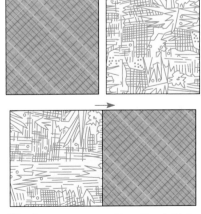

Fig. 3   **Four Patch Unit**

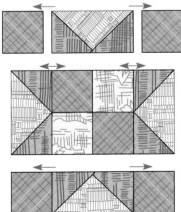

Fig. 4

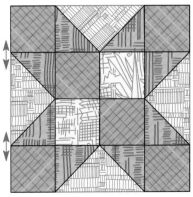

Hearth and Home Block

With its big, bold squares, this block is great to make in lots of different color combinations. You can give it a scrappier look as I have here with lots of fabrics or make it stand out with solid fabrics by using just two colors. You can turn this block into a pillow (see Hearth and Home Pillow, chapter 4) or make it into a mini quilt by following the finishing directions for the Indian Block Mini Quilt in chapter 4.

Finished Block Size: 25" (63.5 cm) square

Materials per block

- Blue print fabrics, 4 fat eighths (each 9" × 21" [23 cm × 53.5 cm])

- Black and white print fabrics, 4 fat eighths (each 9" × 21" [23 cm × 53.5 cm])

- White/gray spot fabric, 1 fat quarter (18" × 21" [45.5 cm × 53.5 cm])

- 5½" (14 cm) Bloc Loc Half-Square Triangle Square Up Ruler (optional)

- Erasable fabric marking pen

CUTTING INSTRUCTIONS

From each of the blue print fabrics, cut:

(2) 5½" (14 cm) squares

(1) 6" (15 cm) square

From each of the black and white print fabrics, cut:

(1) 5½" (14 cm) square

(1) 6" (15 cm) square

From the white/gray spot fabric, cut:

(2) 5½" (14 cm) squares

(1) 5½" × 15½" (14 cm × 39.5 cm) rectangle

1. Following the Half-Square Triangle directions in this chapter, make a Half-Square Triangle using (1) 6" (15 cm) blue square and (1) 6" (15 cm) black and white square. Trim the HSTs to 5½" (14 cm) square (**Figure 1**).

2. In the same manner as step 1, make 6 more HSTs using the remaining 6" (15 cm) blue squares and 6" (15 cm) black and white squares. Make 8 total.

3. Arrange 2 matching HSTs with (1) 5½" (14 cm) black and white print square and (1) 5½" (14 cm) blue square as shown (**Figure 2**).

4. Sew the finished pieces together by row, pressing the seams toward the darker fabric. Then sew the two rows together.

5. Pin and sew (1) 5½" (14 cm) blue square and (1) 5½" (14 cm) white/gray spot square. Press the seams toward the blue fabric (**Figure 3**). Make 2 units total.

6. Pin and sew (1) 5½" (14 cm) blue square to each short end of the 5½" × 15½" (14 cm × 39.5 cm) white/gray spot rectangle. Press the seam towards the blue fabric (**Figure 4**).

7. Arrange the finished units as shown (**Figure 5**).

8. Sew the units together by row, pinning to make sure the seams align and pressing seams open. Sew the rows together, pinning and pressing seams open (**Figure 6**).

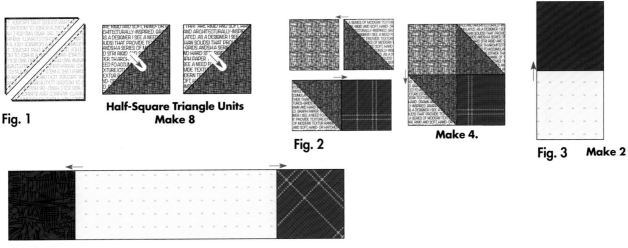

Fig. 1

**Half-Square Triangle Units
Make 8**

Fig. 2

Make 4.

Fig. 3   Make 2

Fig. 4

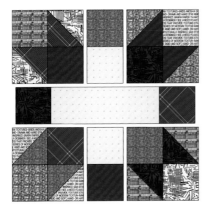

Fig. 5

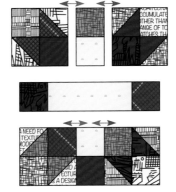

Fig. 6

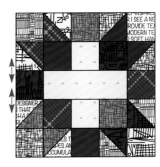

String Block

When making blocks that involve sewing strips on the bias, it is always a good idea to sew them to a foundation fabric as you go, so you do not have a lot of movement or distortion while making them. Here, I used a quilt-as-you-go method, sewing the strips to the batting as I pieced the block. The batting provides the supportive foundation and also lets you quilt your blocks as you make them. If you do not want to sew these String blocks using the quilt-as-you-go method, sew the strips to the foundation fabric of your choice.

Finished size: 12" (30.5 cm) square

Materials per block

- Teal print fabric, 1 fat eighth (9" × 21" [23 cm × 53.5 cm]) (fabric A)

- Lime green print fabrics, 2 fat eighths (each (9" × 21" [23 cm × 53.5 cm]) (fabric B)

- Aqua print fabrics, 2 fat eighths (each (9" × 21" [23 cm × 53.5 cm]) (fabric C)

- White print fabrics, 2 fat eighths (each (9" × 21" [23 cm × 53.5 cm]) (fabric D)

- Light green print fabrics, 2 fat sixteenths (9" × 10½" [23 cm × 26.5 cm]) (fabric E)

- Batting, 13" (33 cm) square

- 12½" (31.5 cm) square ruler

- Erasable fabric marking pen

CUTTING INSTRUCTIONS

From fabric A, cut:
(1) 2½" × 20½" (6.5 cm × 52 cm) strip

From each fabric B, cut:
(1) 2½" × 18½" strip (6.5 cm × 47 cm) strip

From each fabric C, cut:
(1) 2½" × 16½" (6.5 cm × 42 cm) strip

From each fabric D, cut:
(1) 2½" × 13½" (6.5 cm × 34.5 cm) strip

From each fabric E, cut:
(1) 2½" × 8½" (6.5 cm × 21.5 cm) strip

1. Using an erasable fabric marking pen, draw a 2½" (6.5 cm) wide strip through the center of the 13" (33 cm) batting square to help position the first strip (**Figure 1**).

2. Place the fabric A strip in between the marked lines and pin in place (**Figure 2**).

3. Center one of the fabric B strips on the diagonal of fabric A with right sides together and pin in place (**Figure 3**). Sew along the raw edges on the right-hand side, sewing through the batting. Open the fabric and press seams outward (**Figure 4**).

4. In the same manner as step 3, center one of the fabric C strips along the diagonal of fabric B with right sides together and pin in place. Sew along the raw edges on the right-hand side, sewing through the batting. Open the fabric and press the seams outward.

5. Continue in this manner with the fabric D and E strips, pinning each centered strip in place along the raw edges on the right-hand side of the previous strip and sewing through the batting. Press the seams outward (**Figure 5**).

6. Following the progression of steps 3–5, sew the remaining fabric B–E strips on the left-hand side (**Figure 6**).

7. Trim the block to 12½" (31.5 cm) square, making sure the center diagonal is aligned on the 45-degree angle of your ruler so the strips are even (**Figure 7**).

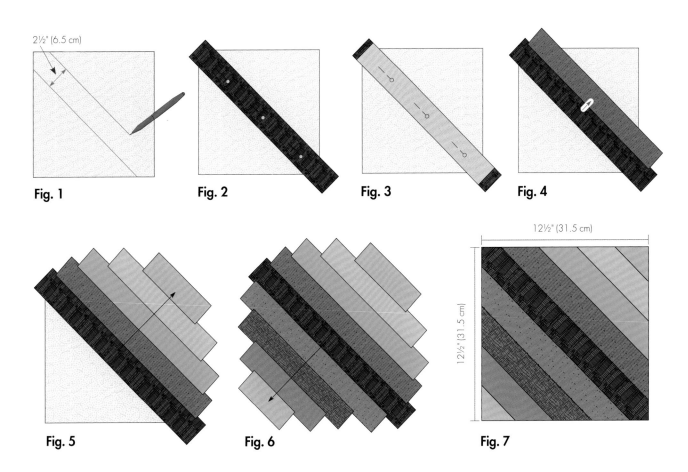

2½" (6.5 cm)

Fig. 1

Fig. 2

Fig. 3

Fig. 4

Fig. 5

Fig. 6

Fig. 7

12½" (31.5 cm)

12½" (31.5 cm)

Indian Block

Using a combination of squares and Half-Square Triangles (HSTs), this block looks great on its own. The geometric pattern also makes a statement when several blocks are used together.

Finished size: 20" (51 cm) square

Materials per block

- White fabric, 1 fat quarter
  (18" × 21" [45.5 cm × 53.5 cm])

- Black fabric, 1 fat quarter
  (18" × 21" [45.5 cm × 53.5 cm])

- Blue fabric, 1 fat quarter
  (18" × 21" [45.5 cm × 53.5 cm])

- Rotary cutter and self-healing mat

- 5½" (14 cm) Bloc Loc Half-Square
  Triangle Square Up Ruler
  (optional)

- Erasable fabric marking pen

CUTTING INSTRUCTIONS

From white fabric, cut:

(4) 6" (15 cm) squares

(2) 5½" (14 cm) squares

From black fabric, cut:

(4) 6" (15 cm) squares

(2) 5½" (14 cm) squares

From blue fabric, cut:

(1) 10½" (26.5 cm) square

1. Using an erasable fabric marking pen, draw a diagonal line from corner to corner on the wrong side of (1) 6" (15 cm) white square. Pin the white square and (1) 6" (15 cm) black square right sides together. Sew along both sides of the marked line with a ¼" (6 mm) seam allowance, then rotary cut along the diagonal line (**Figure 1**).

2. Open both squares. Press seam towards the darker fabric and trim the Half-Square Triangles (HSTs) to 5½" (14 cm) square (**Figure 2**).

3. Repeat steps 1 and 2 with the remaining white and black 6" (15 cm) squares to make 8 HSTs total.

4. Referring to **Figure 3**, lay out the 10½" (26.5 cm) blue square and (4) HSTs as shown, paying attention to the direction

of the diagonal line in the HSTs. Pin and sew each pair of HSTs together, pressing the seam towards the darker fabric.

5. Sew 1 set of HSTs to either side of the blue square. Press seams towards the blue square.

6. Referring to **Figure 4**, arrange (1) 5½" (14 cm) black square, (2) HSTs, and (1) 5½" (14 cm) white square along the top of the blue center block and the remaining squares and HSTs along the bottom as shown, paying attention to the direction of the diagonal line in the HSTs.

7. Pin and sew each row together, pressing seams towards the darker fabric. Sew these rows to the top and bottom of the center block, pressing seams outwards (**Figure 5**).

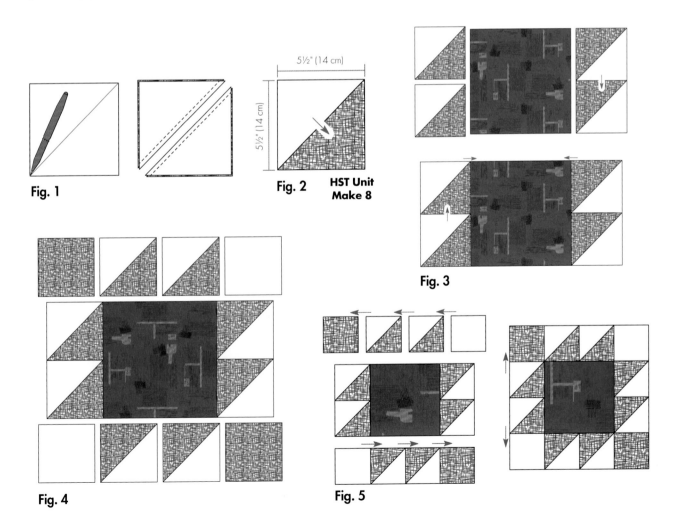

5½" (14 cm)

5½" (14 cm)

Fig. 1

Fig. 2

HST Unit Make 8

Fig. 3

Fig. 4

Fig. 5

CHAPTER 4

QUILTS AND PROJECTS

With lots of bold designs and blocks to choose from, you will find loads of quilts and smaller sized projects to make in this chapter. While the blocks themselves may be steeped in tradition, fabric choices and patterns give you very modern ways to make your quilts and projects stand out.

HALF-SQUARE TRIANGLES

Quilt

Maybe you have been holding onto a layer cake of fabric. If so, this project is perfect for turning that stack of squares into a lovely quilt. The large 9" (23 cm) Half-Square Triangle blocks are just right for using up a bundle of your favorite fabric range, or you can mix and match colors with ease to find the perfect combination. Given its size, this quilt comes together relatively quickly. Universal in appeal, this charming quilt is perfect for children or adults alike. You can use a solid piece of fabric for the backing or sew the featured pieced backing (see chapter 5).

Finished Quilt Size: 72½" (184 cm) square
Finished Block Size: 9" (23 cm) square

LAYER CAKE AND FAT QUARTER FRIENDLY

Materials

- Pink print fabrics, 4 fat quarters
  (each 18" × 21" [45.5 cm × 53.5 cm])

- Jade green print fabrics, 4 fat quarters
  (each 18" × 21" [45.5 cm × 53.5 cm])

- Turquoise print fabrics, 4 fat quarters
  (each 18" × 21" [45.5 cm × 53.5 cm])

- Lime green print fabrics, 4 fat quarters
  (each 18" × 21" [45.5 cm × 53.5 cm])

- Floral print background fabric, 2½ yards (2.3 m)

- Backing fabric, 80" (203 cm) square (or
  optional pieced backing in chapter 5)

- Binding fabric, ⅝ yard (57 cm)

- Batting, 80" (203 cm) square

- 12½" (31.5 cm) square ruler or
  12½" (31.5 cm) Bloc Loc Half-Square
  Triangle Square Up Ruler (optional)

- Erasable fabric marking pen

Cutting Instructions

*From each of the pink, jade green,
turquoise, and lime green fabrics, cut:*

(2) 10" (25.5 cm) squares (you will have 32

squares total)

*From the floral print background
fabric, cut:*

(8) 10" (25.5 cm) × WOF (width-of-fabric)
strips; subcut into (32) 10" (25.5 cm) squares

From the binding fabric, cut:

(8) 2½" (6.5 cm) × WOF strips

*All seam allowances are ¼" (6 mm)
unless otherwise indicated.*

1. Following the Half-Square Triangle block directions in chapter 3, make (64) 9" (23 cm) Half-Square Triangle blocks using the background fabric and all of the colored print squares (**Figure 1**). You will have 16 HST blocks each in pink, jade green, turquoise and lime green.

2. Referring to **Figure 2**, arrange the blocks as shown.

◢ *Tip:* Take your time arranging the prints in each color group so they are evenly balanced.

3. Pin and sew the blocks together in each row, pressing the odd row seams to the left and the even row seams to the right (**Figure 3**).

4. Pin and sew each of the long rows together, taking your time when pinning these rows so the seams "nest." Press the seams down.

5. Layer the backing (wrong-side up), the batting, and the quilt top (right-side up); baste the layers together. Quilt as desired. (The featured quilt was professionally longarm quilted.)

6. Bind the quilt. (For tips and directions on finishing your quilt, turn to chapter 1.)

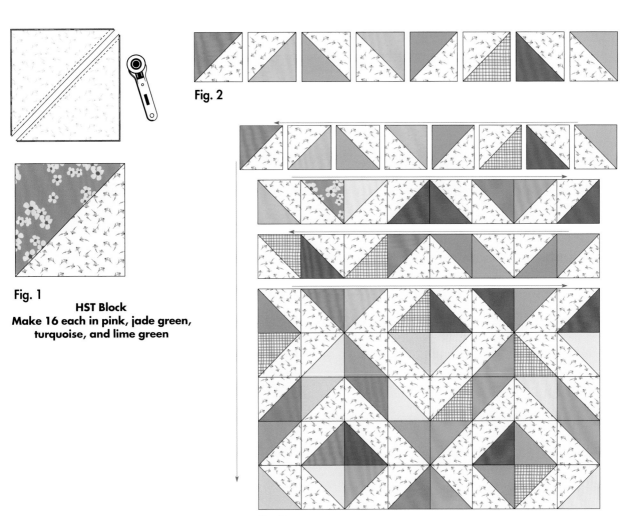

Fig. 1
HST Block
Make 16 each in pink, jade green, turquoise, and lime green

Fig. 2

Fig. 3

FLYING GEESE Quilt

This is the perfect quilt to showcase those large-scale prints you have been looking forward to using. Pick fabrics with contrasting colors that stand out from the background to make your quilt even more eye-catching.

Finished Quilt Size: 60½" (153.5 cm)

Finished Block Size: 20" (51 cm)

Materials

- Floral fabrics, 4 fat quarters
  (each 18" × 21" [45.5 cm × 53.5 cm])

- Spot fabrics, 4 fat quarters
  (each 18" × 21" [45.5 cm × 53.5 cm])

- Green floral fabric, 2½ yards (2.3 m)

- Gray background fabric, 3½ yards (3.2 m)

- Binding fabric, ½ yard (45.5 cm)

- Batting, 68" (172.5 cm) square

- Backing fabric, 68" (172.5 cm) square

FAT QUARTER FRIENDLY

Cutting Instructions

From each of the floral and spot fabrics, cut:

(1) 10¾" × 20¾" (27.5 cm × 52.5 cm) rectangle

From the green floral fabric, cut:

(6) 10¾" (27.5 cm) × WOF (width-of-fabric) strips; subcut into (16) 10¾" (27.5 cm) squares.

(2) 10½" (26.5 cm) × WOF strips; subcut into (4) 10½" (26.5 cm) squares.

From the gray background fabric, cut:

(6) 10¾" (27.5 cm) × WOF strips; subcut into (16) 10¾" (27.5 cm) squares

(4) 10¾" (27.5 cm) × WOF strips; subcut into (8) 10¾" × 20¾" (27.5 cm × 52.5 cm) rectangles

From the binding fabric, cut:

(7) 2½" (6.5 cm) × WOF strips

All seam allowances are ¼" (6 mm) unless otherwise indicated.

Binding Tip

Sometimes when you use excessively busy prints for your borders, it can become difficult to choose a binding fabric that works with your quilt top. One of my favorite solutions is to use the same fabric for the binding that you used for the borders. This can make a perfect finishing touch so all of the fabrics in your quilt flow together seamlessly.

How to Use Excess Fabric

When trimming your Flying Geese, you will have lots of "excess corners." Save these excess corners and use them to make a pieced backing for your quilt (see chapter 5 for inspiration). This will add great interest to your quilt and help use up any excess fabric left over from your quilt top.

Another idea: Turn the excess corners into Half-Square Triangles and make a coordinating pillow (see the Scrappy HST Pillow in this chapter).

1. Following the instructions in chapter 3, make 1 Flying Geese Block from each of the (8) 10¾" × 20¾" (27.5 cm × 52.5 cm) floral and spot fabric rectangles and the (16) 10¾" (27.5 cm) gray squares.

2. Arrange the four Flying Geese with the blocks oriented as shown (**Figure 1**).

3. Sew each of the rows together, pinning and pressing toward the horizontal Flying Geese. Sew the top and bottom row together, pinning the "nesting" seams (**Figure 2**).

Refer to **Figure 3** throughout assembly.

4. Make 8 single Flying Geese units using the (8) 10¾" × 20¾" (27.5 cm × 52.5 cm) gray background rectangles and the (16) 10¾" (27.5 cm) green floral squares. Trim the units to 10½" × 20½" (26.5 cm × 52 cm). Sew two units together along the short ends. Repeat to make 4 side borders.

5. Arrange the Flying Geese side borders and the (4) 10½" (26.5 cm) green floral fabric squares around the center block as shown.

6. For the top and bottom border, sew a 10½" (26.5 cm) square to either side of the Flying Geese units. Sew the left and right side borders to the center block. Pin and press seams towards the center Flying Geese block.

7. Sew the top and bottom borders and press seams open in the middle and towards the floral squares.

8. Layer the backing (wrong side up), the batting, and the quilt top (right-side up); baste together. Quilt as desired. (The featured quilt was professionally longarm quilted.)

9. Bind the quilt. (For tips and detailed directions on finishing your quilt, turn to chapter 1).

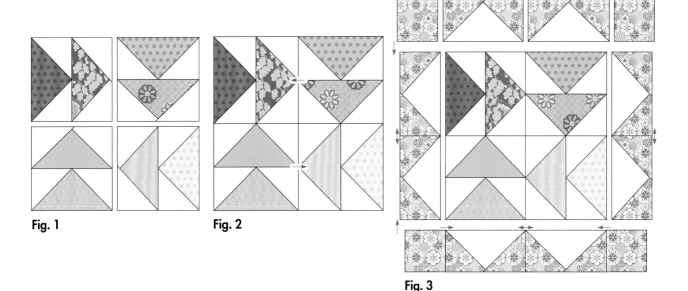

Fig. 1   Fig. 2

Fig. 3

LOZENGE
Quilt

With its graphic design, this quilt is perfect for a bedroom with modern style. It is also a great project for maximizing your stash because you can mix and match fabrics for both the backgrounds and the Lozenge blocks. So go ahead, break out those low-volume scraps and fat quarter bundles you've been holding onto to make this charming quilt.

Finished Quilt Size: 72½" × 84½" (184 cm × 214.5 cm)

Finished Block Sizes: 24" (61 cm) square, 12" (30.5 cm) square, 6" (15 cm) square

FAT QUARTER FRIENDLY

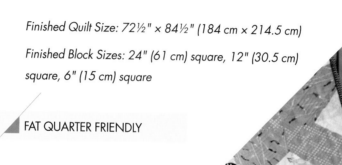

Materials

- Aqua print fabric, 4 fat quarters
  (each 18" × 21" [45.5 cm × 53.5 cm])

- Blue print fabric, 4 fat quarters
  (each 18" × 21" [45.5 cm × 53.5 cm])

- Pink print fabric, 4 fat quarters
  (each 18" × 21" [45.5 cm × 53.5 cm])

- Green print fabric, 2 fat quarters
  (each 18" × 21" [45.5 cm × 53.5 cm])

- Orange print fabric, 2 fat quarters
  (each 18" × 21" [45.5 cm × 53.5 cm])

- Black print fabric, 2 fat quarters
  (each 18" × 21" [45.5 cm × 53.5 cm])

- Red print fabric, 2 fat quarters
  (each 18" × 21" [45.5 cm × 53.5 cm])

- Dark blue print fabric, 2 fat quarters
  (each 18" × 21" [45.5 cm × 53.5 cm])

- Mint print fabric, 2 fat quarters
  (each 18" × 21" [45.5 cm × 53.5 cm])

- Purple print fabric, 2 fat eighths
  (each 9" × 21" [23 cm × 53.5 cm])

- Yellow print fabric, 2 fat eighths
  (each 9" × 21" [23 cm × 53.5 cm])

- Teal print fabric, 2 fat eighths
  (each 9" × 21" [23 cm × 53.5 cm])

- Coral print fabric, 2 fat eighths
  (each 9" × 21" [23 cm × 53.5 cm])

- Gray background fabrics, 4 (each ½ yard
  [45.5 cm])

- Cream background fabrics, 4 (each ½ yard
  [45.5 cm])

- Backing fabric, 80" × 92" (203 cm × 233.5 cm)

- Binding fabric, ⅝ yard (57 cm)

- Batting, 80" × 92" (203 cm × 233.5 cm)

- 12½" (31.5 cm) square ruler

- Erasable fabric marking pen

Cutting Instructions

From each of the aqua, blue, and pink prints, cut:
(1) 12½" (31.5 cm) square

From each of the green, orange, black, red, dark blue, and mint prints, cut:
(4) 6½" (16.5 cm) squares

From each of the purple, yellow, teal, and coral prints, cut:
(8) 3½" (9 cm) squares

From each of 4 gray and 4 cream background fabrics, cut:
(3) 6½" (16.5 cm) squares (24 total for large Lozenge blocks)
(12) 3½" (9 cm) squares (96 total for medium Lozenge blocks)
(16) 1½" (3.8 cm) squares (128 total for small Lozenge blocks)

From each of 3 gray and 3 cream background fabrics, cut:
(2) 12½" (31.5 cm) squares

From the remaining 1 gray and 1 cream background fabrics, cut:
(1) 12½" (31.5 cm) square

From the binding fabric, cut:
(8) 2½" (6.5 cm) × WOF (width-of-fabric) strips

All seam allowances are ¼" (6 mm) unless otherwise indicated.

◢ Tip: As an alternative to the gray or cream background fabric, you can substitute (8) low-volume background fabrics (each ½ yard [45.5 cm]).

1. Following the instructions in chapter 3, make 3 large Lozenge blocks using the (24) 6½" (16.5 cm) background fabric squares and the (12) 12½" (31.5 cm) squares: 4 aqua, 4 pink, and 4 blue squares. Make 1 large Lozenge block (4 Lozenge units in each) in each color, so you have 1 pink, 1 blue, and 1 aqua block (**Figure 1**). These blocks will measure 24½" (62 cm) unfinished.

2. To make the 12 medium Lozenge Blocks, gather the (96) 3½" (9 cm) background fabric squares and the (48) 6½" (16.5 cm) print squares in green, orange, black, red, dark blue, and mint prints. Following the Lozenge block directions, make (2) 12½" (31.5 cm) Lozenge blocks in each color (**Figure 2**).

3. To make the 4 small Lozenge blocks, gather the (128) 1½" (3.8 cm) background fabric squares and the (32) 3½" (9 cm) print squares in purple, yellow, teal, and coral. In the same manner as the previous steps, make (4) 6½" (16.5 cm) unfinished Lozenge blocks in each color. Gather 1 small Lozenge block in each color, then pin and sew them together in a 2 × 2 formation, pressing seams open (**Figure 3**). These blocks measure 12½" (31.5 cm) unfinished.

4. Referring to **Figure 4**, arrange the small, medium, and large Lozenge blocks and the (14) 12½" (31.5 cm) background squares as shown. Pin and sew the blocks together by row, pressing the seams open.

Note: You may want to change the position of some of the blocks to achieve a more balanced look.

5. Sew the long rows together, pinning and pressing as you go.

6. Layer the backing (wrong-side up), the batting, and the quilt top (right-side up); baste the layers together. Quilt as desired. (The featured quilt was professionally longarm quilted.)

7. Bind the quilt. (For tips and detailed directions on finishing your quilt, turn to chapter 1.)

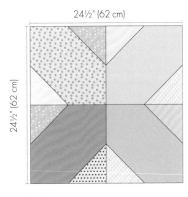

Fig. 1

24½" (62 cm)

24½" (62 cm)

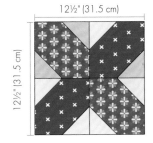

Fig. 2

12½" (31.5 cm)

12½" (31.5 cm)

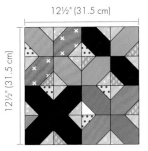

Fig. 3

12½" (31.5 cm)

12½" (31.5 cm)

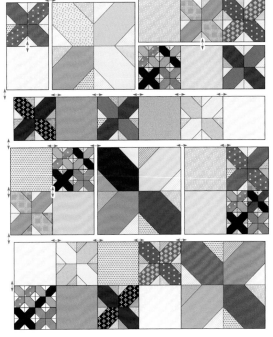

Fig. 4

BOW TIE Quilt

You can make this striking quilt with a limited number of colors against one background fabric as shown here or make it full of prints with low volume background fabrics. Whichever you choose, this quilt will simply look fabulous. There are many different arrangements with Bow Tie blocks; here is one of my favorites.

Finished Quilt Size: 60½" × 80½" (153.5 cm × 204 cm)

Finished Block Size: 20" (51 cm) square

FAT QUARTER FRIENDLY

Materials

- Black print fabrics, 6 fat quarters
  [each 18" × 21" (45.5 cm × 53.5 cm)]

- Gray print fabrics, 6 fat quarters
  [each 18" × 21" (45.5 cm × 53.5 cm)]

- Taupe print fabrics, 6 fat quarters
  [each 18" × 21" (45.5 cm × 53.5 cm)]

- Black and white print fabrics, 6 fat quarters
  [each 18" × 21" (45.5 cm × 53.5 cm)]

- White background fabric,
  2¼ yards (2.1 m)

- Backing fabric, 68" × 88"
  (172.5 cm × 223.5 cm)

- Binding fabric, ⅝ yard (57 cm)

- Batting, 68" × 88" (172.5 cm × 223.5 cm)

- Erasable fabric marking pen

Cutting Instructions

From each of the black, gray, taupe, and black/white fabrics, cut:

(4) 5½" (14 cm) squares

(4) 3" (7.5 cm) squares

From the white background fabric, cut:

(14) 5½" (14 cm) × WOF (width-of-fabric) strips; subcut into (96) 5½" (14 cm) squares

From the binding fabric, cut:

(8) 2½" (6.5 cm) × WOF strips

All seam allowances are ¼" (6 mm) unless otherwise indicated.

1. Following the directions for the Bow Tie block in chapter 3, make (12) 20" (51 cm) Bow Tie blocks using the black, gray, taupe and black/white print fabrics as shown in each individual block (**Figure 1**).

2. Arrange the blocks in 4 rows with 3 blocks each. Take your time to arrange the blocks, being careful to rotate them in the correct direction to have the same color fabrics run on the diagonal.

3. Pin and sew the blocks together by row, pressing the seams in the odd rows to the left and the even rows to the right (**Figure 2**).

4. Pin and sew the 4 rows together, taking your time pinning the rows to make sure the seams "nest" (the seams will lay together in opposite directions to distribute the bulk). Press the seams down.

5. Layer the backing (wrong-side up), the batting, and the quilt top (right-side up); baste the layers together. Quilt as desired. (The featured quilt was professionally longarm quilted.)

6. Bind the quilt. (For tips and directions on finishing your quilt, turn to chapter 1.)

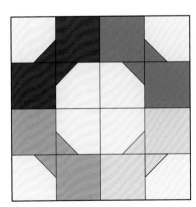

Fig. 1

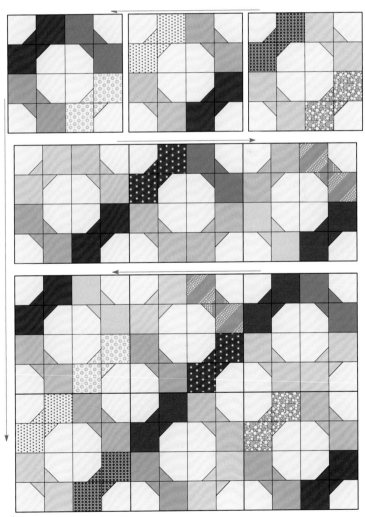

Fig. 2

LOG CABIN
Quilt

Once you have mastered Log Cabin blocks, making this inspiring quilt will be a fun way to build your skills. It's also a great project to use up favorite fabrics from your stash as well as lovely coordinates. The featured design includes a pieced back (see chapter 5). You can also use the fabric of your choice (dimensions are included in the materials list).

Finished Quilt Size: 60" × 72½" (152.5 cm × 184 cm)
Finished Block Size: 24" (61 cm) square

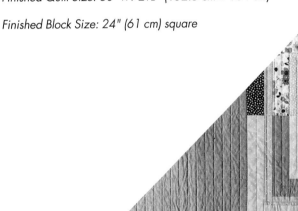

Materials

- Large floral print fabric, ⅓ yard (30.5 cm)

- Purple spot print fabric, ¼ yard (23 cm)

- Blue cross print fabric, ⅜ yard (34.5 cm)

- Yellow spot print fabric, ⅜ yard (34.5 cm)

- Peach mini hearts print fabric, ¼ yard (23 cm)

- Blue sprinkle dot print fabric, ⅓ yard (30.5 cm)

- Peach cross print fabric, ⅙ yard (15.5 cm)

- Blue mini heart print fabric, ⅛ yard (11.5 cm)

- Small floral print fabric, 1 fat quarter (18" × 21" [45.5 cm × 53.5 cm])

- Peach screen print fabric, ⅙ yard (15.5 cm)

- Chambray background fabric, 2¼ yards (2.1 m)

- Backing fabric, 68" × 80" (172.5 cm × 203 cm) (or optional pieced backing in chapter 5)

- Binding fabric, ½ yard (45.5 cm)

- Batting, 68" × 80" (172.5 cm × 203 cm)

- Rotary cutter and self-healing mat

- 12½" (31.5 cm) square ruler

- Erasable fabric marking pen

Cutting Instructions

For Block 1, cut:

(1) 11" (28 cm) square from large floral print

(2) 2½" × 11" (6.5 cm × 28 cm) strips and (2) 2½" × 15" (6.5 cm × 38 cm) strips from purple spot print

(2) 2½" × 15" (6.5 cm × 38 cm) strips and (2) 2½" × 19" (6.5 cm × 48.5 cm) strips from blue cross print

(2) 1½" × 19" (3.8 cm × 48.5 cm) strips and (2) 1½" × 21" (3.8 cm × 53.5 cm) strips from yellow spot print

(2) 2½" × 21" (6.5 cm × 53.5 cm) strips and (2) 2½" × 25" (6.5 cm × 63.5 cm) strips from peach mini hearts print

For Block 2, cut:

(1) 11" (28 cm) square from blue sprinkle dot print

(2) 2½" × 11" (6.5 cm × 28 cm) strips and (2) 2½" × 15" (6.5 cm × 38 cm) strips from peach cross print

(2) 2½" × 15" (6.5 cm × 38 cm) strips and (2) 2½" × 19" (6.5 cm × 48.5 cm) strips from large floral print

(2) 1½" × 19" (3.8 cm × 48.5 cm) strips and (2) 1½" × 21" (3.8 cm × 53.5 cm) strips blue mini hearts print

(2) 2½" × 21" (6.5 cm × 53.5 cm) strips and (2) 2½" × 25" (6.5 cm × 63.5 cm) strips blue cross print

For Block 3, cut:

(1) 11" (28 cm) square from small floral print

(2) 2½" × 11" (6.5 cm × 28 cm) strips and (2) 2½" × 15" (6.5 cm × 38 cm) strips from peach screen print

(2) 2½" × 15" (6.5 cm × 38 cm) strips and (2) 2½" × 19" (6.5 cm × 48.5 cm) strips from blue sprinkle dot print

(2) 1½" × 19" (3.8 cm × 48.5 cm) strips and (2) 1½" × 21" (3.8 cm × 53.5 cm) strips from purple spot print

(2) 2½" × 21" (6.5 cm × 53.5 cm) strips and (2) 2½" × 25" (6.5 cm × 63.5 cm) strips from yellow spot print

From the chambray fabric, cut:

(1) 14½" × 72½" (37 cm × 184 cm) strip from the length of fabric

(1) 22" × 72½" (56 cm × 184 cm) strip from the length of fabric

From the binding fabric, cut:

(7) 2½" (6.5 cm) × WOF (width-of-fabric) strips

All seam allowances are ¼" (6 mm) unless otherwise indicated.

1. Following the instructions in chapter 3, make 3 Log Cabin blocks using the cutting instructions for this quilt to determine the combinations of fabric featured in each finished block (**Figure 1**). Blocks measure 25" (63.5 cm) square unfinished.

2. Using an erasable fabric marking pen and a ruler, divide block 1 into 4 quarters. Make sure the lines are even, then rotary cut the block into four pieces (**Figure 2**). Repeat this step for block 2 and block 3.

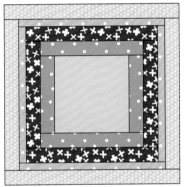
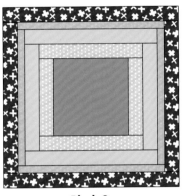
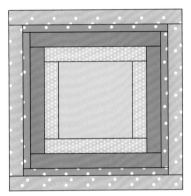

Block 1 **Block 2** **Block 3**

Fig. 1

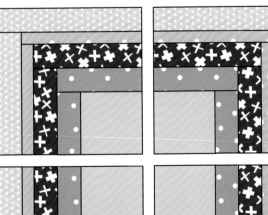

Fig. 2

3. Arrange the 12 Log Cabin pieces in a 2 × 6 formation, rotating the pieces in different directions as shown in **Figure 3**.

◢ Tip: Take your time to create a nice balance of prints and colors.

4. Pin and sew the first row together, taking your time to match up intersecting seams. Press seams open. Repeat for the second row (**Figure 4**).

5. Pin and sew the first and second rows together to make a complete block. This re-pieced block should measure 24½" (62 cm) square.

6. In the same manner, join rows three and four to make a block, then join rows five and six to make a block.

Sew together each of the 3 re-pieced Log Cabin blocks to make a 24½" × 72½" (62 cm × 184 cm) long row (**Figure 5**).

7. Pin and sew the 14½" × 72½" (37 cm × 184 cm) chambray background strip to the left side of the Log Cabin blocks. Pin and sew the sew 22" × 72½" (56 cm × 184 cm) chambray background strip to the right. Press the seams toward the background fabric.

8. Layer the backing (wrong-side up), the batting, and the quilt top (right-side up); baste the layers together. Quilt as desired. (The featured quilt was professionally longarm quilted).

9. Bind the quilt. (For tips and detailed directions on finishing your quilt, turn to chapter 1.)

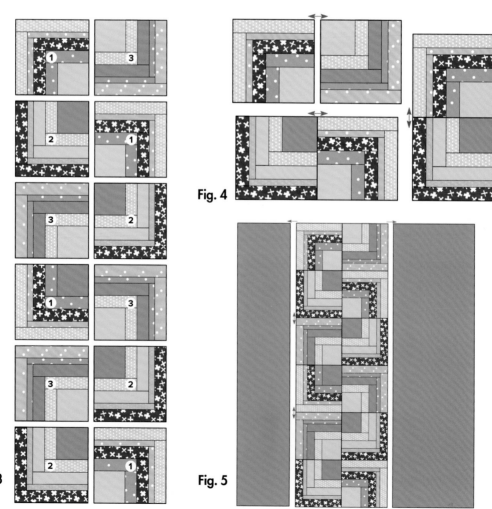

Fig. 3

Fig. 4

Fig. 5

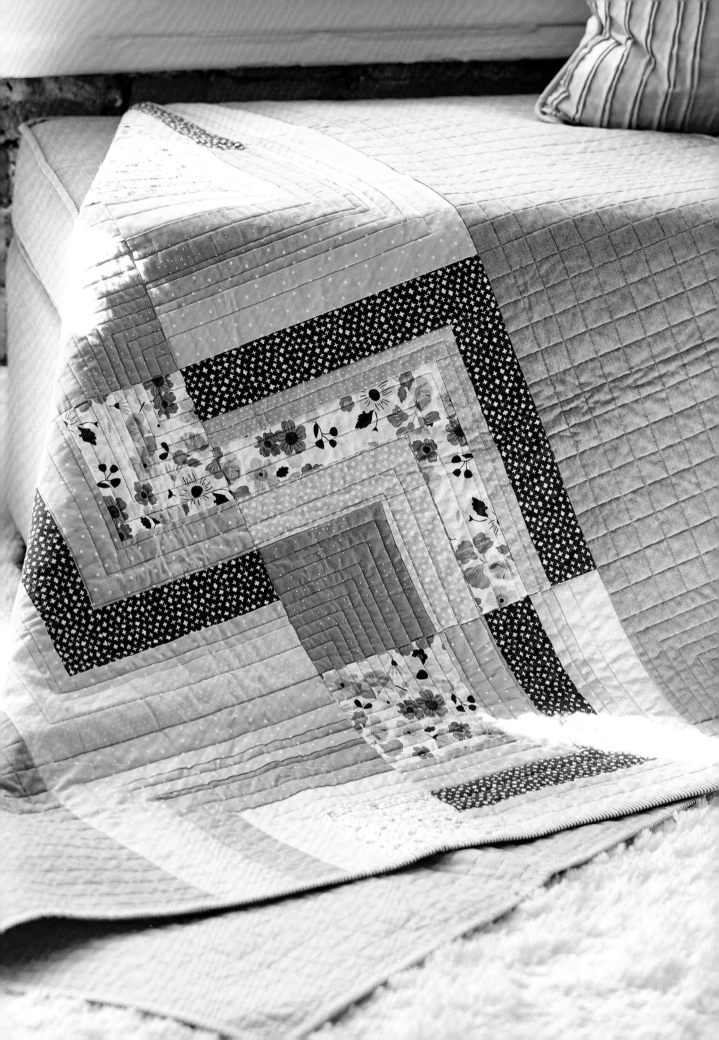

SIMPLEX STAR Quilt

As this design shows, a simple block can make a sophisticated statement. With its large blocks and coordinating color palette, this bed-size quilt will complement any room. For a completely different look, replace the Simplex Star block with one of the other 24" (61 cm) blocks in this book, including the Lozenge, Churn Dash, Indian Star, String, Scrappy HST, and Sarah's Choice blocks.

Finished Quilt Size: 96½" (245 cm) square
Finished Block Size: 24" (61 cm) square

Materials

- Dark blue fabric, 1⅛ yard (1 m)

- Medium blue fabric, 2 yards (1.8 m)

- Light blue fabric, 1⅝ yards (1.5 m)

- Gray background fabric, 4½ yards (4.1 m)

- Backing fabric, 105" (266.5 cm) square

- Binding fabric, ¾ yard (70 cm)

- Batting, 105" (266.5 cm) square

- 12½" (31.5 cm) square ruler

- Erasable fabric marking pen

Cutting Instructions

From the dark blue fabric, cut:

(16) 9" (23 cm) squares

From the light blue fabric, cut:

(16) 9" (23 cm) squares

(8) 8½" (21.5 cm) squares

From the medium blue fabric, cut:

(32) 8½" (21.5 cm) squares

From the gray background fabric, cut:

(6) 24½" × WOF (width-of-fabric) (62 cm × WOF) strips; subcut into:

(4) 24½" × 13½" (62 cm × 34.5 cm) strips for piece A

(2) 24½" × 30½" (62 cm × 77.5 cm) strips for piece B

(2) 24½" × 5½" (62 cm × 14 cm) strips for piece C

(2) 24½" × 21½" (62 cm × 54.5 cm) strips for piece D

(2) 24½" × 14½" (62 cm × 37 cm) strips for piece E

From the binding fabric, cut:

(10) 2½" (6.5 cm) × WOF strips

All seam allowances are ¼" (6 mm) unless otherwise indicated.

1. Following the instructions in chapter 3, make 8 Simplex Star blocks (**Figure 1**). The blocks will measure 24½" (62 cm) square.

2. Referring to **Figure 2**, arrange the 8 Simplex Star blocks and the gray background fabric pieces A-E as shown. Sew the blocks together in long columns, pinning and pressing fabrics towards the gray background fabric as you go.

3. Sew each of the long columns together, taking your time to pin them so you can line up the seams from the Simplex Star blocks. Press the seams open.

4. Layer the backing (wrong-side up), the batting, and the quilt top (right-side up); baste the layers together. Quilt as desired. (The featured quilt was professionally longarm quilted.)

5. Bind the quilt. (For tips and detailed directions on finishing your quilt, turn to chapter 1.)

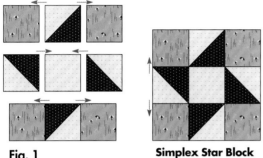

Fig. 1   **Simplex Star Block**

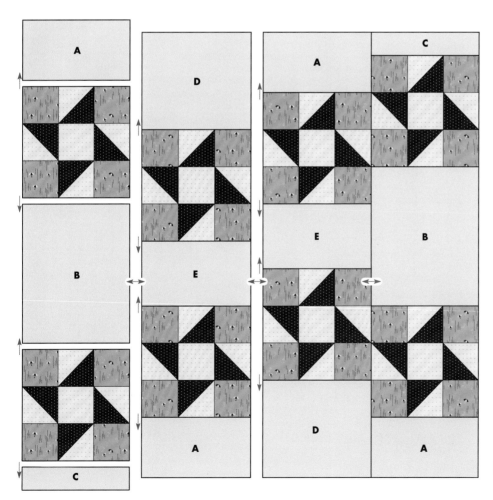

Fig. 2

CHURN DASH Quilt

I love using feature prints as the star of a quilt design. The print used here was the basis for pulling the other fabric color choices. When you use a print that has lots of colors in it, you can choose fabrics to match in one colorway as I have done here or use several colors that coordinate.

To make this quilt as shown, turn to chapter 5 for the quilt back design.

Finished Quilt Size: 56½" (143.5 cm) square

Finished Block Size: 24" (61 cm) square

Materials

- Peach print fabrics, (4) ⅓ yard (30.5 cm) each

- Multicolor print fabric, ½ yard (45.5 cm)

- White/gold spot background fabric, 2¼ yards (2.1 m)

- Backing fabric, 64" (162.5 cm) square (or optional pieced backing in chapter 5)

- Binding fabric, ½ yard (45.5 cm)

- Batting, 64" (162.5 cm) square

- 12½" (31.5 cm) square ruler

- Erasable fabric marking pen

Cutting Instructions

From each of the peach fabrics, cut:

(2) 9" (23 cm) squares

(4) 4½" × 8½" (11.5 cm × 21.5 cm) rectangles

From the multicolor print fabric, cut:

(1) 4½" (11.5 cm) × WOF (width-of-fabric) strip; subcut into (4) 4½" × 8½" (11.5 cm × 21.5 cm) rectangles

(2) 9" (23 cm) squares

(1) 8½" (21.5 cm) square

From the white/gold spot background fabric, cut:

(1) 8½" (21.5 cm) × WOF strip; subcut into (4) 8½" (21.5 cm) squares

(5) 4½" (11.5 cm) × WOF strips; subcut into (20) 4½" × 8½" (11.5 cm × 21.5 cm) rectangles

(2) 8½" (21.5 cm) × WOF strips; subcut into (4) 8½" × 16½" (21.5 cm × 42 cm) rectangles

(3) 9" (23 cm) × WOF strips; subcut into (10) 9" (23 cm) squares

From the binding fabric, cut:

(6) 2½" (6.5 cm) × WOF strips

All seam allowances are ¼" (6 mm) unless otherwise indicated.

1. Following the Churn Dash block directions in chapter 3 and using 9" (23 cm) squares, make a 24" (61 cm) Churn Dash block using 3 HSTs with peach and background fabric and 1 HST made with the multicolor print and background fabric (**Figure 1**). Trim the blocks to 8½" (21.5 cm) square. Make 4 blocks total.

◢ Tip: To make the 4 multicolor print HSTs, use (2) 9" (23 cm) multicolor print squares and (2) 9" (23 cm) background squares. For each Churn Dash block, replace one of the peach/background print HSTs with a multicolor print and background HST. Save the extra peach/background HST for another project or quilt back.

2. To make a sashing row, gather (1) 8½" × 16½" (21.5 cm × 42 cm) background rectangle, (1) 4½" × 8½" (11.5 cm × 21.5 cm) multicolor print rectangle, and (1) 4½" × 8½" (11.5 cm × 21.5 cm) background rectangle.

Referring to **Figure 2**, place the two smaller rectangles right sides together, then pin and sew along the long edge. Pin and sew the rectangles to the larger background rectangle along the width. Make 4 sashing strips total.

3. Referring to **Figure 3**, arrange the Churn Dash blocks, sashing rows, and the 8½" (21.5 cm) multicolor print square as shown. Pin and sew each row, taking your time to match up the points. Press the seams open.

4. Sew all of the rows together along the long edges, pinning and pressing the seams open as you go.

5. Layer the backing (wrong-side up), the batting, and the quilt top (right-side up); baste the layers together. Quilt as desired. (The featured quilt was professionally longarm quilted.)

6. Bind the quilt. (For tips and directions on finishing your quilt, turn to chapter 1.)

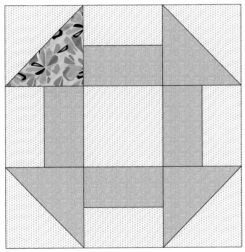

Fig. 1   **Churn Dash Block**
              Make 4

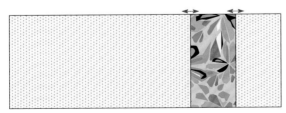

Fig. 2   **Sashing Strip**
                Make 4

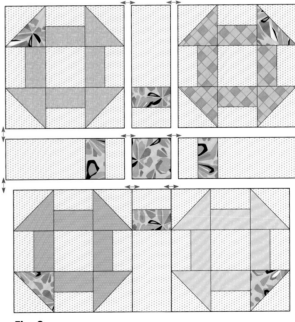

Fig. 3

HOME TREASURE
Quilt

This quilt would make a stunning picnic blanket for a spring gathering in the park. It's made from a supersized Home Treasure block, a traditional design that is usually sewn up at about 15" (38 cm) square. If you are looking to make a quilt in a short time frame, this design is perfect.

Finished Quilt Size: 60½" (153.5 cm) square
Finished Block Size: 60" (152.5 cm) square

Materials

- Aqua print fabric, 1 fat quarter (18" × 21" [45.5 cm × 53.5 cm])

- Floral print fabric, 1½ yards (1.4 m)

- Pink print fabric, ½ yard (45.5 cm)

- White/navy spot background fabric, 1¾ yards (1.6 m)

- Backing fabric, 68" (172.5 cm) square

- Binding fabric, ½ yard (45.5 cm)

- Batting, 68" (172.5 cm) square

- Rotary cutter and self-healing mat

- 12½" (31.5 cm) square ruler

- 24" (61 cm) long quilting ruler

- Erasable fabric marking pen

Cutting Instructions

From the aqua fabric, cut:

(1) 15½" (39.5 cm) square for the center block

From the floral fabric, cut:

(2) 16" (40.5 cm) squares; subcut in half on the diagonal

(4) 16½" (42 cm) squares; subcut in half on the diagonal

From the pink print fabric, cut:

(4) 8" × 15½" (20.5 cm × 39.5 cm) rectangles

From the white/navy spot background fabric, cut:

(4) 15½" (39.5 cm) squares

(2) 11½" (29 cm) squares; subcut in half on the diagonal for the center block

(2) 11¾" (30 cm) squares; subcut in half on the diagonal

(4) 8⅜" (21.5 cm) squares; subcut in half on the diagonal

From the binding fabric, cut:

(7) 2½" (6.5 cm) × WOF (width of fabric) strips

All seam allowances are ¼" (6 mm) unless otherwise indicated.

Cutting and Sewing on the Bias

This quilt is made with many blocks that are cut on the bias. Make sure to use lots of pins while preparing them so you don't stretch your blocks as you sew them together. Because of the bias cuts in these triangles, I oversized some of the triangles. By trimming them down to the correct size after sewing, your results will be more accurate than cutting them exactly. The stretch of the bias can distort the shape of your triangle, especially after ironing, so press gently.

1. Gather the 15½" (39.5 cm) aqua square and the (4) 11½" (29 cm) white/navy spot triangles. Fold 1 white/navy spot triangle in half to make a crease along the longest side. On each side of the aqua square fold and mark a light center crease. Place a white/navy spot triangle on one side of the aqua square with right sides together, matching up the center creases and raw edges. Pin in place. Sew along the pinned side, pressing the seam toward the aqua square (**Figure 1**).

◢ Note: The triangle tips will extend past the square, but you will need this seam allowance shortly.

2. In the same manner as step 1, sew another 11½" (29 cm) white/navy background triangle on the opposite side of the square. Sew the remaining triangles on opposite sides of the square (**Figure 2**). Trim the tips. The block should measure 21½" (54.5 cm) square.

3. In the same manner as steps 1 and 2, sew the (4) 16" (40.5 cm) floral print triangles to the center square unit (**Figure 3**). Trim the tips. The block should measure 30½" (77.5 cm) square.

4. Gather a 8" × 15½" (20.5 cm × 39.5 cm) pink print rectangle and (2) 8⅜" (21.5 cm) white/navy spot triangles. Line up a triangle on the bottom right corner of one rectangle as shown (the tip will extend past the rectangle at the top) and pin in place (**Figure 4**). Sew the edge with a ¼" (6 mm) seam allowance and press the seam outwards. Repeat with a second white/navy spot triangle on the left-hand side (**Figure 5**).

5. Place one of the 11¾" (30 cm) white/navy spot triangles along the long top edge of the pink rectangle with right sides together and pin in place (**Figure 6**). Sew with a ¼" (6 mm) seam allowance and press the seam outwards (**Figure 7**).

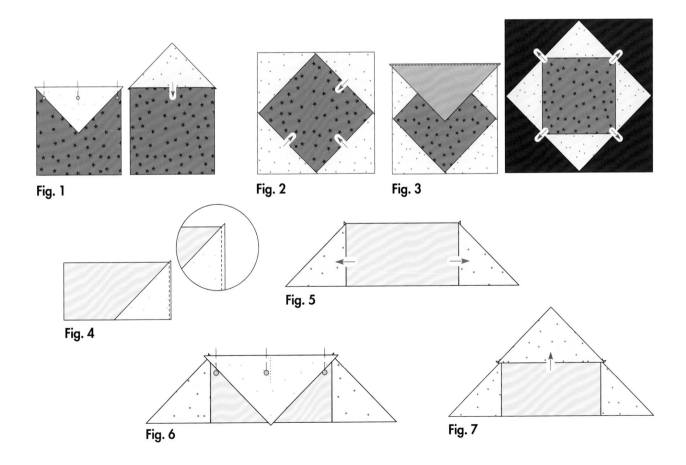

Fig. 1 Fig. 2 Fig. 3

Fig. 4 Fig. 5

Fig. 6 Fig. 7

6. Turn the pink rectangle unit wrong-side up. Using an erasable fabric marking pen and the 24" (61 cm) long quilting ruler and lining up the bottom angle from the bottom corner as shown, mark a straight 45-degree line and trim any excess fabric (**Figure 8**).

⚠ *Note: The excess fabric will mainly be along the top triangle.*

7. Fold one of the 16½" (42 cm) floral print triangles in half along the longer edge to make a center crease. Fold the pink rectangle unit in half along one of the shorter sides and mark a center crease. With right sides together, line up the center crease marks and pin the raw edges together along this side as shown (**Figure 9**). (The floral fabric triangle will extend past both corners.) Sew the triangle in place along this seam with a ¼" (6 mm) seam allowance and press the seam toward the floral fabric. Repeat for the other side (**Figure 10**). Trim the rectangle to 15½" × 30½" (39.5 cm × 77.5 cm), making sure you have included the seam allowance at the rectangle-triangle intersection.

8. Repeat steps 4–7 to make 4 pink and floral rectangle units total.

9. Arrange the center square unit, pink and floral rectangle units, and 15½" (39.5 cm) white/navy spot squares as shown (**Figure 11**).

10. Pin and sew the finished pieces together by row, taking time to match up the points. Press the seams open. Then sew the long rows together, pinning and pressing as you go.

11. Layer the backing (wrong-side up), the batting, and the quilt top (right-side up); baste the layers together. Quilt as desired. (The featured quilt was professionally longarm quilted.)

12. Bind the quilt. (For tips and detailed directions on finishing your quilt, turn to chapter 1.)

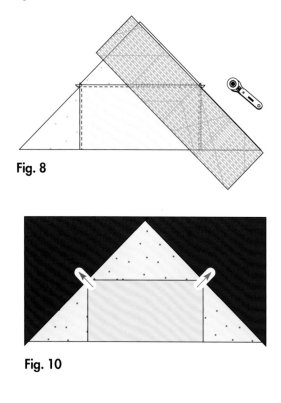

Fig. 8

Fig. 10

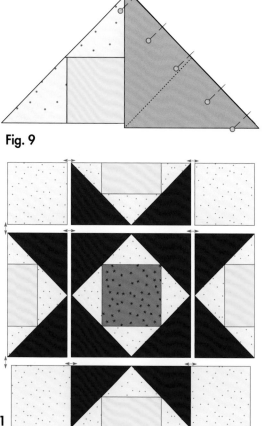

Fig. 9

Fig. 11

STRING BLOCK Pillow

This complex-looking, envelope-back pillow is easier to make than it looks and sews up quickly, especially when you use the "quilt-as-you-go" method detailed in the String Block directions in chapter 3. With this design, you can choose fabrics that stick to a specific color scheme to complement any room in your house or use up scraps for a completely different look.

Finished Pillow Size: 24" (61 cm) square

◢ FAT QUARTER FRIENDLY

Materials

- Gray/purple/aqua main print fabric, 1 fat quarter (18" × 21" [45.5 cm × 53.5 cm]) (fabric A)

- Aqua/white print fabric, 2 fat quarters (each 18" × 21" [45.5 cm × 53.5 cm]) (fabric B)

- Gray print fabric, 2 fat quarters (each 18" × 21" [45.5 cm × 53.5 cm]) (fabric C)

- Purple print fabric, 2 fat quarters (each 18" × 21" [45.5 cm × 53.5 cm]) (fabric D)

- White print fabric, 2 fat quarters (each 18" × 21" [45.5 cm × 53.5 cm]) (fabric E)

- Backing fabric, ¾ yard (68.5 cm)

- Batting, (4) 13" (33 cm) squares

- Pillow insert, 26" (66 cm) square (I used the large pillow from Ikea)

- 12½" (31.5 cm) square ruler

- Erasable fabric marking pen

Cutting Instructions

From fabric A, cut:

(4) 2½" × 20½" (6.5 cm × 52 cm) strips

From each of the fabric B prints, cut:

(4) 2" × 18½" (6.5 cm × 47 cm) strips

From each of the fabric C prints, cut:

(4) 2½" × 16½" (6.5 cm × 42 cm) strips

From each of the fabric D prints, cut:

(4) 2½" × 13½" (6.5 cm × 34.5 cm) strips

From each of the fabric E prints, cut:

(4) 2½" × 8½" (6.5 cm × 21.5 cm) strips

From the backing fabric, cut:

(2) 19" × 24½" (49.5 cm × 62 cm) rectangles

All seam allowances are ¼" (6 mm) unless otherwise indicated.

1. Following the directions in chapter 3, make 4 String blocks.

2. Arrange the String blocks as shown in a 2 × 2 formation so the main print is intersecting (**Figure 1**).

◢ Note: You can orient the blocks in any direction you choose to create different patterns.

3. Pin and sew the blocks together by row, pressing the seams open. Then pin and sew the top and bottom rows together, pressing seam open.

4. Quilt the pillow top by machine or hand. (The featured pillow was machine quilted with metallic thread using the *V* shape made by the strips.) Set your completed pillow top aside.

5. To make the pillow backing, fold over ½" (1.3 cm) of the raw edge along one long side and press. Fold under another 1" (2.5 cm) and press. Machine stitch the open side closed ⅛" (3 mm) in from the fold, then along the folded edge. Repeat for the second piece (**Figure 2**).

6. Place the pillow top right-side up and place one backing piece on top with right sides together, matching the raw edges at the bottom and sides of the pillow front (**Figure 3**). Arrange the second backing piece so it is overlapping the first pillow back piece with right sides together, matching the raw edges at the top and sides. Pin around the outside of your pillow (**Figure 4**).

7. Sew around the outside raw edges of your pillow with a ¼" (6 mm) seam allowance. Overlock or zig-zag stitch the raw edges. Turn your finished pillow out the right way and fill with the insert.

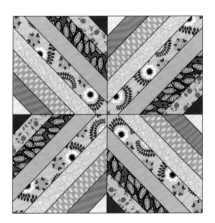

Fig. 1

Fig. 2

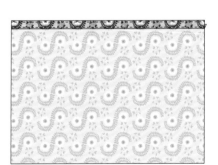

Fig. 3

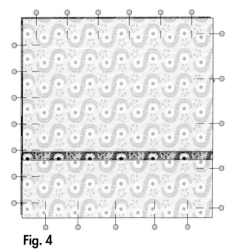

Fig. 4

LOLA Quilt

Featuring giant blocks, this quilt is quick to make so you can be snuggled up with it sooner rather than later. I love how the negative space in this quilt allows the blocks to do the talking. There's also a beautiful pieced backing (see chapter 5) or you can use the fabric dimensions below to create a back with your favorite fabric.

Finished Quilt Size: 70½" × 74½" (179 cm × 189 cm)

Finished Block Sizes: 42" (106.5 cm) and 28" (71 cm)

Materials

- Blue floral print fabric, ½ yard (45.5 cm)

- Blue and white spot print fabric, ½ yard (45.5 cm)

- Gray print fabric, ¾ yard (68.5 cm)

- White mini heart background fabric, 3½ yards (3.2 m)

- Backing fabric, 78" × 83" (198 cm × 211 cm) (or optional pieced backing in chapter 5)

- Binding fabric, ⅝ yard (57 cm)

- Batting, 78" × 83" (198 cm × 211 cm)

- Rotary cutter and self-healing mat

- 24" (61 cm) long quilting ruler

Cutting Instructions

From the blue floral print, cut:

(1) 8" (20.5 cm) strip × WOF (width of fabric); subcut into (4) 8" (20.5 cm) squares

(1) 5½" (14 cm) strip × WOF; subcut into (6) 5½" (14 cm) squares

From the blue and white spot print, cut:

(1) 8" (20.5 cm) strip × WOF; subcut into (4) 8" (20.5 cm) squares

(1) 5½" (14 cm) strip × WOF; subcut into (8) 5½" (14 cm) squares

From the gray print, cut:

(1) 15½" (39.5 cm) strip × WOF; subcut into (4) 8" × 15½" (20.5 cm × 39.5 m) rectangles

(1) 10½" (26.5 cm) strip × WOF; subcut into (4) 5½" × 10½" (14 cm × 26.5 cm) rectangles

From the white background fabric cut:

(1) 29½" × 70½" (75 cm × 179 cm) strip from the length of fabric for piece A

(1) 3½" × 42½" (9 cm × 108 cm) strip from the length of fabric for piece B

(2) 22⅛" (56 cm) strips × WOF; subcut each strip into (1) 22⅛" (56 cm) square and (1) 15⅛" (38.5 cm) square, then cut each square in half on the diagonal

(2) 7½" × 14½" (19 cm × 37 cm) rectangles for piece C

(2) 10½" × 14½" (26.5 cm × 37 cm) rectangles for piece D

From the binding fabric, cut:

(8) 2½" (6.5 cm) × WOF strips

All seam allowances are ¼" (6 mm) unless otherwise indicated.

1. Following the Lola block instructions in chapter 3, make 1 large Lola block using the (4) 8" (20.5 cm) blue floral squares, (4) 8" (20.5 cm) blue and white spot squares, (4) 8" × 15½" (20.5 cm × 39.5 cm) gray rectangles, and the 22⅛" (56 cm) background triangles. The unfinished block should measure 42½" (108 cm) square (**Figure 1**).

2. Create a Four Patch unit following the Lola block instructions with the (2) 5½" (14 cm) blue floral squares and (2) 5½" (14 cm) blue and white spot squares.

3. Arrange the Four Patch unit, (1) 5½" (14 cm) blue floral square, (2) 5½" (14 cm) blue and white spot squares, and (2) 5½" × 10½" (14 cm × 26.5 cm) gray rectangles as shown (**Figure 2**).

4. Referring to **Figure 3**, sew the pieces together as follows. Pin and sew (1) 5½" (14 cm) blue and white spot square to the short side of the gray rectangle with right sides together, pressing the seam toward the blue square. Pin and sew this strip to the top of the Four Patch block, lining up the gray rectangle with the top of the Four Patch as shown. Sew the 5½" (14 cm) blue floral to one short end of the gray rectangle and the 5½" (14 cm) blue and white square to the other. Press the seams outwards. Pin and sew this strip to the other side of the Four Patch block, lining up the seams.

◢ Note: The blue and white spot square will extend past the Four Patch.

5. Using the quilting ruler and rotary cutter, trim the block on the diagonal with a ¼" (6 mm) seam allowance through the diagonal of the Four Patch and blue and white spot squares (**Figure 4**).

Fig. 1

Fig. 2

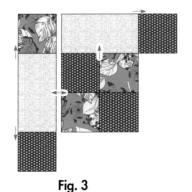

Fig. 3

Fig. 4

6. Following the Lola block instructions, pin and sew the 15⅛" (38.5 cm) background triangle with right sides together on one side of the block. Repeat on the second side (**Figure 5**). Press the seams open and trim the block to 14½" × 28½" (37 cm × 72.5 cm).

7. Repeat steps 2–6 to make a second half small Lola block.

8. Referring to **Figure 6**, assemble the quilt top:

• Sew background piece B to the bottom of the large Lola Block; press the seam open.

• Orient 1 small Lola block with the Four Patch facing to the right, then pin and sew 1 piece C to the top and 1 piece D to the opposite end, pressing seams open.

• In the same manner, orient the other small Lola block with the Four Patch to the left, then sew 1 piece C to the top and 1 piece D to the opposite end, pressing the seams open.

• Sew the pieces together as shown, pinning to match up the seams and pressing seams open.

• Pin and sew piece A to the top of the Lola blocks piece and press the seams open.

9. Layer the backing (wrong-side up), the batting, and the quilt top (right-side up); baste the layers together. Quilt as desired. (The featured quilt was professionally longarm quilted.)

10. Bind the quilt. (For tips and detailed directions on finishing your quilt, turn to chapter 1.)

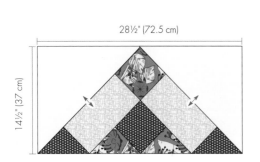

28½" (72.5 cm)

14½" (37 cm)

Fig. 5

Lola Half-Block Make 2

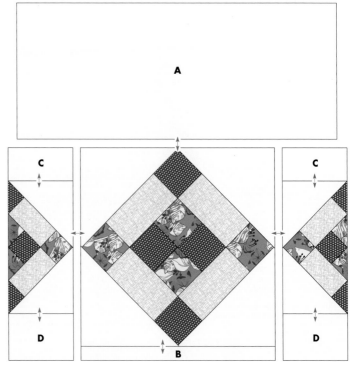

Fig. 6

CONSTELLATION SAMPLER Quilt

Learning to make basic quilt blocks is a great way to increase your skills and improve your sewing. In chapter 3, I covered a variety of star blocks. Here I combined five of them into one gorgeous quilt pattern. This was a fun project to design. The large-scale florals and tone-on-tone prints along with a variety of medium-scale prints offered the perfect color palette and fabrics to create with. I love texture, so the background fabric is a beautiful yarn dye with a metallic thread. It creates a great contrast against the bright and bold star fabrics.

Finished Quilt Size: 70½" × 80½" (179 cm × 204.5 cm)

Finished Block Sizes:

Millennium block: 30" (76 cm) square

Ohio Star block: 15" (38 cm) square

Rising Star block: 20"
(51 cm) square

Sarah's Choice block: 24"
(61 cm) square

Missouri Star block: 20"
(51 cm) square

Materials

- Gold 1 fabric, ⅓ yard (30.5 cm)

- Gold 2 fabric, ¼ yard (23 cm)

- Gold 3 fabric, ¼ yard (23 cm)

- Gold 4 fabric, ½ yard (45.5 cm)

- Gold 5 fabric, ½ yard (45.5 cm)

- Red fabrics, 5 fat sixteenths
  (each 9" × 10½" [23 cm × 26.5 cm])

- Blue 1 fabric, 1 fat quarter
  (18" × 21" [45.5 cm × 53.5 cm])

- Blue 2 fabric, 1 fat eighth
  (9" × 21" [23 cm × 53.5 cm])

- Blue 3 fabric, 1 fat quarter
  (18" × 21" [45.5 cm × 53.5 cm])

- Blue 4 fabric, ⅓ yard (30.5 cm)

- Purple 1 fabric, ¼ yard (23 cm)

- Purple 2 fabric, ¼ yard (23 cm)

- Green 1 fabric, 1 fat eighth
  (9" × 21" [23 cm × 53.5 cm])

- Green 2 fabric, 1 fat eighth
  (9" × 21" [23 cm × 53.5 cm])

- Green 3 fabric, ⅓ yard (30.5 cm)

- Cream background fabric, 4 yards (3.7 m)

- Backing fabric, 78" × 88"
  (198 cm × 223.5 cm)

- Binding fabric, ¾ yard (68.5 cm)

- Batting, 78" × 88" (198 cm × 223.5 cm)

- Erasable fabric marking pen

- 12½" (31.5 cm) square ruler

- Quilting rulers: 5" × 10" (12.5 cm × 25.5 cm)
  Bloc Loc Ruler Flying Geese Square Up Ruler;
  6" × 12" (15 cm × 30.5 cm) Bloc Loc Flying
  Geese Square Up Ruler; 6½" (16.5 cm)
  Bloc Loc Half-Square Triangle Square Up
  Ruler (optional)

Cutting Instructions

The cutting instructions for each of the blocks can be found in the specific block directions in chapter 3. You will need one of each block (use the cream background fabric listed here in place of any background fabrics in the block directions).

◢ Note: Cut pieces B, F and A first from the length of fabric, then cut remaining pieces.

From the cream background fabric, cut:

(2) 22" (56 cm) squares; cut in half on the diagonal once (this is the Millennium on-point background)

(1) 4½" × 42½" (11.5 cm × 108 cm) strip (Piece A*)

(1) 5½" × 46½" (14 cm × 118 cm) strip (Piece B*)

(1) 9½" × 15½" (24 cm × 39.5 cm) strip (Piece C)

(1) 12½" × 24½" (31.5 cm × 62 cm) strip (Piece D)

(1) 4½" × 20½" (11.5 cm × 52 cm) strip (Piece E)

(1) 13½" × 46½" (34.5 cm × 118 cm) strip (Piece F*)

(1) 20½" × 26½" (52 cm × 67.5 cm) strip (Piece G)

(1) 9½" × 24½" (24 cm × 62 cm) strip (Piece H)

From the binding fabric, cut:

(9) 2½" (6.5 cm) × WOF (width-of-fabric) strips

All seam allowances are ¼" (6 mm) unless otherwise indicated.

◢ Pinning Tip

When working with large pieces of fabric, make sure you take your time to pin the pieces correctly. Here's how: Fold and mark creases at the center and quarter points (¼ and ¾) in the pieces, then match these up with the corresponding pieces at the marked creases. Pin at the creases, then add more pins between these points. This will ensure your fabric is distributed evenly when you are working with longer and bulkier pieces.

1. Following the directions in chapter 3, make (1) each of the Millennium block, Ohio Star block, Rising Star block, Sarah's Choice block, and Missouri Star block.

2. Turn the Millennium block on-point by sewing (1) 22" (55.5 cm) background fabric triangle to each side of the Millennium Block (this is done in the same way as the Missouri Star block; see chapter 3 for detailed directions) (**Figure 1**). The block should measure 42½" (108 cm) square. Trim, if needed.

3. Using **Figure 2** as your guide, arrange the background pieces A-H along with each of your completed star blocks as shown.

4. Sew the blocks together in two halves:

• Sew the first half in the following order: Sew piece A to the left side of the Millennium block. Sew piece B to the top of piece A and the Millennium block. Sew piece F to the bottom of the Millennium block, then sew piece G to the left side of the Missouri Star block. Sew this row to the piece containing the Millennium block. Press all seams open.

• Sew the second half in this order: Sew piece C to the left-hand side of the Ohio Star block. Sew piece D to the bottom of piece C and the Ohio Star block. Sew piece E to the left-hand side of the Rising Star block and sew both to the bottom of the piece containing the Ohio Star block. Sew Sarah's Choice to piece H and then sew this piece to piece E and the Rising Star block. Press all seams open.

5. Sew the two halves of the quilt together and press the seam open.

6. Layer the backing (wrong-side up), the batting, and the quilt top (right-side up); baste the layers together. Quilt as desired. (The featured quilt was professionally longarm quilted.)

7. Bind the quilt. (For tips and detailed directions on finishing your quilt, turn to chapter 1.)

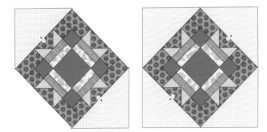

Fig. 1

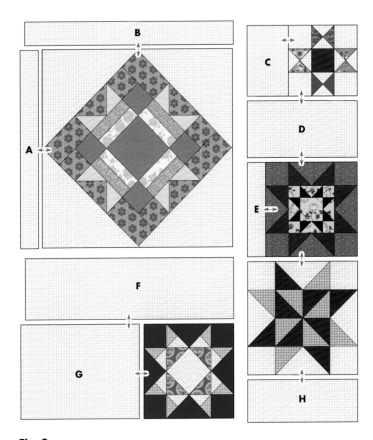

Fig. 2

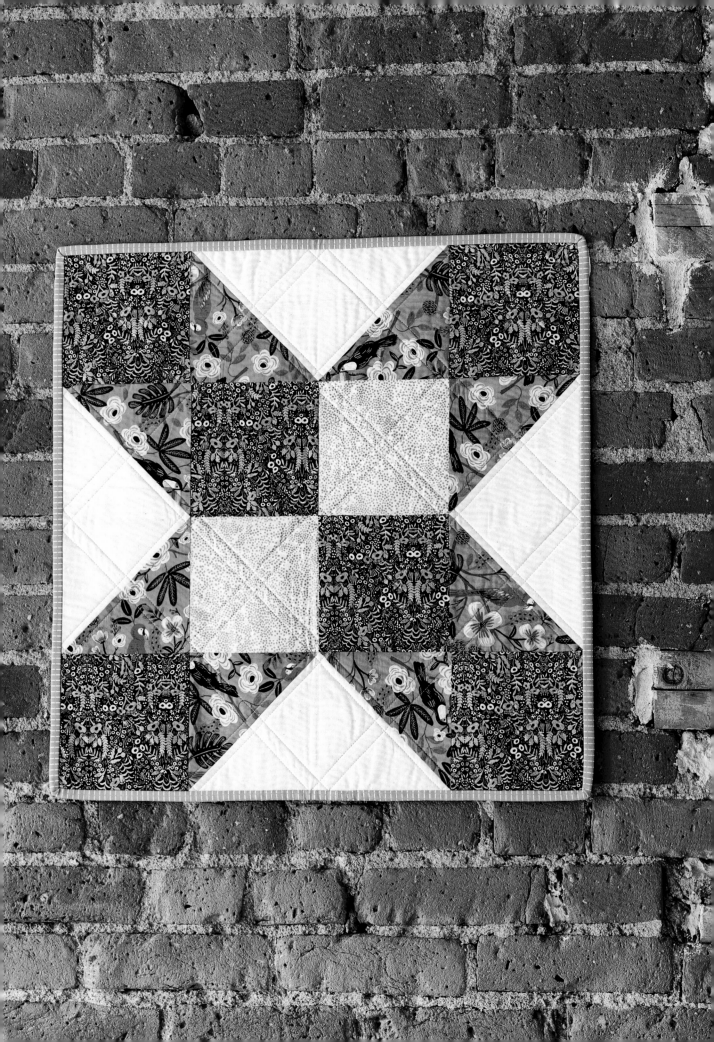

INDIAN STAR MINI
Quilt

Big and bold, this mini quilt makes a statement. It would look great hanging in a hallway, living room, or in your sewing space. You can also turn it into a stunning floor pillow by following the finishing directions in the String Heart Pillow.

Finished Mini Quilt Size: 24½" (62 cm) square

Finished Block Size: 24" (61 cm) square

Materials

- Coral fabric, ⅜ yard (34.5 cm)

- Black fabric, ¼ yard (23 cm)

- Gold fabric, 1 fat eighth (9" × 21" [23 cm × 53.5 cm])

- Cream background fabric, ⅜ yard (34.5 cm)

- Backing fabric, 30" (76 cm) square

- Binding fabric, ¼ yard (23 cm)

- Hanging sleeve fabric ⅛ yard (11.5 cm)

- Batting, 30" (76 cm) square

Cutting Instructions

From the coral fabric, cut:

(8) 6¾" (17 cm) squares

From the black fabric, cut:

(6) 6½" (16.5 cm) squares

From the gold fabric, cut:

(2) 6½" (16.5 cm) squares

From the cream background fabric, cut:

(4) 6¾" × 12¾" (17 cm × 32.5 cm) rectangles

From the binding fabric, cut:

(3) 2½" (6.5 cm) × WOF (width-of-fabric) strips

All seam allowances are ¼" (6 mm) unless otherwise noted.

Mix and Match

This mini quilt can easily be made with one of the other 24" (61 cm) blocks in this book, including the Churn Dash, Lozenge, and Simplex Star.

1. Following the instructions in chapter 3, make 1 Indian Star block (**Figure 1**).

2. Layer the backing (wrong-side up), the batting, and the mini quilt top (right-side up); baste the layers together. Quilt as desired. (The featured mini quilt was machine quilted by sewing cross-hatched lines following the diagonals in the Flying Geese blocks all over).

3. To make a hanging sleeve for your mini quilt, cut a 4" × 23½" (10 cm × 59.5 cm) rectangle from the hanging sleeve fabric (**Figure 2**). Fold each short end ¼" (6 mm)

toward the wrong side of the fabric and press. Topstitch these shorter sides at ⅛" (3 mm). Press the rectangle in half lengthwise with wrong sides together and raw edges aligned. Turn your quilted mini quilt wrong-side up and pin the raw edge of the hanging sleeve into the top seam allowance on the mini quilt. Sew in place to hold. Handsew the bottom folded edge into place along the back of the mini quilt to allow for a hanger to be run through this sleeve (**Figure 3**).

4. Bind the mini quilt. (For tips and detailed directions on finishing your quilt, turn to chapter 1).

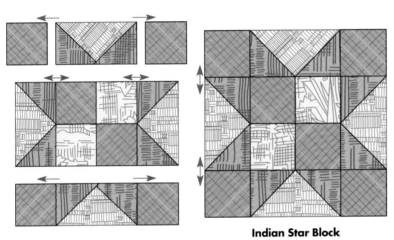

Indian Star Block

Fig. 1

Fig. 2

Fig. 3

HEARTH & HOME Pillow

Pillows are a quick project that can easily transform any space or piece of furniture, such as a chair, couch, or bed, in no time. This Hearth and Home pillow looks great on its own or sew up a few to make your space even more inviting. It also includes directions for inserting a zipper back.

Finished Pillow Size: 25" (63.5 cm) square

Materials

- Aqua print fabrics, 4 fat eighths (each 9" × 21" [23 cm × 53.5 cm])

- Gray print fabrics, 4 fat eighths (each 9" × 21" [23 cm × 53.5 cm])

- Gray spot fabric, 1 fat quarter (18" × 21" [45.5 cm × 53.5 cm])

- Backing fabric, ¾ yard (68.5 cm)

- Batting, 30" (76 cm)

- Pillow insert, 26" (66 cm) (I used the large pillow inserts from Ikea)

- Zipper, 25" (63.5 cm)

- 5½" (14 cm) Bloc Loc Half-Square Triangle Square Up Ruler (optional)

- Erasable fabric marking pen

- Zipper foot

Cutting Instructions

From each of the aqua print fabrics, cut:

(2) 5½" (14 cm) squares

(1) 6" (15 cm) square

From each of the gray print fabrics, cut:

(1) 5½" (14 cm) square

(1) 6" (15 cm) square

From the gray spot fabric, cut:

(2) 5½" (14 cm) squares

(1) 5½" × 10½" (14 cm × 26.5 cm) rectangle

From the backing fabric, cut:

(1) 9" × 25½" (23 cm × 65 cm) rectangle

(1) 19" × 25½" (48.5 cm × 65 cm) rectangle

All seam allowances are ¼" (6 mm) unless otherwise indicated.

Plump that Pillow

For plumper, fuller-looking pillows, use a pillow insert that is one size larger than the finished pillow size.

Hearth and Home block

1. Following the instructions in chapter 3, make a Hearth and Home block.

2. Layer the batting and pillow top right-side up; baste them together. Quilt as desired. (The featured pillow was machine quilted with 1" [2.5 cm] grid lines.) Trim the batting to size.

3. To make the pillow backing, set the smaller piece of backing fabric wrong-side up. Referring to **Figure 1**, fold over ⅜" (1 cm) of the raw edge along one long side and press. Fold over another 1" (2.5 cm) and press. Set this top piece aside.

4. Set the larger piece of backing wrong-side up. Fold over ⅜" (1 cm) of the raw edge along one long side and press. Place the zipper face-up on a work surface. With the backing fabric right-side up, align the folded edge with the zipper edge as shown and pin the fold in place (**Figure 2**). Open the zipper a few inches.

5. Put the zipper foot on your sewing machine. Guide the edge of the foot to sew along the edge of the zipper. When you reach the zipper, place the needle down into the fabric, then lift up the presser foot and move the zipper pull past the machine foot. Put the presser foot back down and continue sewing to the end (**Figure 3**).

6. Set both pieces of backing fabric on a work surface wrong-side up. Align the folded edge of the smaller backing fabric (top piece) with the unsewn zipper edge and pin (**Figure 4**).

7. Sew along the edge of the zipper, moving the zipper pull and sewing as close to the zipper edge as you can (**Figure 5**).

8. With right sides together, sew the completed pillow back to the pillow as shown (**Figure 6**).

9. Turn the pillow right-side out (**Figure 7**). Fill with the insert.

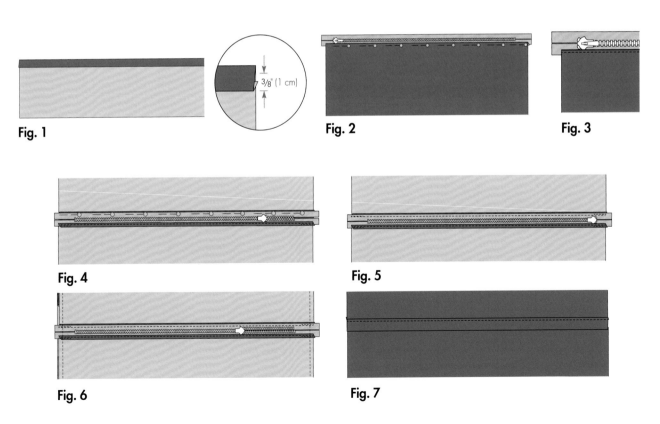

Fig. 1

⅜" (1 cm)

Fig. 2

Fig. 3

Fig. 4

Fig. 5

Fig. 6

Fig. 7

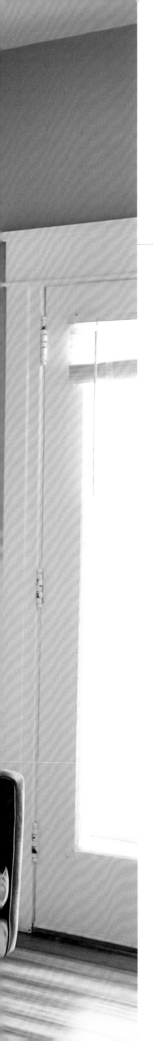

STRIP
HEART Quilt

Making a quilt is truly a gift from the heart. With its big, bold design, this colorful Strip Heart quilt is a perfect gesture to show how much you care. It's also fat quarter-friendly, so it is a great excuse to use up any favorite fabric bundles you have been saving for a special occasion. I chose a rayon lawn as the background for this pattern. It is very fine and delicate, so it was helpful to turn off the steam on my iron when pressing the rayon lawn. The drape in this fabric works well with the cotton fabrics, so do not feel afraid to mix up different fabrics in the same project.

Finished Quilt Size: 54½" × 72½" (138.5 cm × 184 cm)

Finished Block Size: 18" (45.5 cm) square

FAT QUARTER FRIENDLY

Pieced Backing Option

When trimming the Flying Geese in this book, you will be left with excess corner triangles. Save these excess corners and use them in the pieced backing as shown in chapter 5. This will add an interesting detail to your quilt and help you use up any excess fabric left over from your quilt top. Another idea: Turn the excess into Half-Square Triangles and make a coordinating pillow to go with your quilt (see the Scrappy Half-Square Triangle Pillow for directions).

Materials

- Pink assorted print fabrics, 4 fat quarters (each 18" × 21" [45.5 cm × 53.5 cm])
- Blue assorted print fabrics, 4 fat quarters (each 18" × 21" [45.5 cm × 53.5 cm])
- Teal assorted print fabrics, 4 fat quarters (each 18" × 21" [45.5 cm × 53.5 cm])
- Green spot print fabric, 1 fat eighth (9" × 21" [23 cm × 53.5 cm])
- Blue mosaic print fabric, 1 fat eighth (9" × 21" [23 cm × 53.5 cm])
- Mustard print fabric, ½ yard (45.5 cm)
- White feather print fabric, ½ yard (45.5 cm)
- White background fabric, 2¾ yards (2.5 m)
- Backing fabric, 62" × 80" (157.5 cm × 203 cm) (or optional pieced backing in chapter 5)
- Binding fabric, ½ yard (45.5 cm)
- Batting, 62" × 80" (157.5 cm × 203 cm)
- 12½" (31.5 cm) square ruler
- Erasable fabric marking pen

Cutting Instructions

From each of 3 pink fabrics, cut:
(1) 9¾" × 18¾" (25 cm × 47.5 cm) rectangle

(2) 5¼" × 9¾" (13.5 cm × 25 cm) rectangles

From 1 pink fabric, cut:
(3) 5¼" × 9¾" (13.5 cm × 25 cm) rectangles

(2) 5¼" (13.5 cm) squares

(1) 5½" (14 cm) square

From each of 3 blue fabrics, cut:
(1) 9¾" × 18¾" (25 cm × 47.5 cm) rectangle

(2) 5¼" × 9¾" (13.5 cm × 25 cm) rectangles

From the remaining blue fabric, cut:
(3) 5¼" × 9¾" (13.5 cm × 25 cm) rectangles

(2) 5¼" (13.5 cm) squares

(1) 5½" (14 cm) square

From the 4 teal fabrics, cut:
(1) 9¾" × 18¾" (25 cm × 47.5 cm) rectangle

(2) 5¼" × 9¾" (13.5 cm × 25 cm) rectangles

From the green spot and blue mosaic fabrics, cut:
(2) 3" × 5¼" (7.5 cm × 13.5 cm) rectangles

(1) 5¼" × 9¾" (13.5 cm × 25 cm) rectangle

(1) 2¾" × 9½" (7 cm × 24 cm) rectangle

From the mustard fabric, cut:
(5) 2¾" (7 cm) × WOF (width-of-fabric) strips; subcut into (10) 2¾" × 18½" (7 cm × 47 cm) rectangles

(4) 2¾" × 5" (7 cm × 12.5 cm) rectangles

From the white feather print fabric, cut:
(5) 2¾" (7 cm) × WOF strips; subcut into (10) 2¾" × 18½" (7 cm × 47 cm) rectangles

(4) 2¾" × 5" (7 cm × 12.5 cm) rectangles

(8) 3" (7.5 cm) squares

From the white background fabric, cut:
(6) 9¾" (25 cm) × WOF strips; subcut into (24) 9¾" (25 cm) squares

(7) 5¼" (13.5 cm) × WOF strips; subcut into (52) 5¼" (13.5 cm) squares (48 for the Strip Heart blocks and 4 extra for the Double Strip Heart block)

(2) 5½" (14 cm) squares

(4) 5" (12.5 cm) squares

From the binding fabric, cut:
(7) 2½" (6.5 cm) × WOF strips

All seam allowances are ¼" (6 mm) unless otherwise indicated.

1. Following the instructions in chapter 3, make 3 pink Strip Heart blocks, 3 blue Strip Heart blocks, and 4 teal Strip Heart blocks (**Figure 1**).

2. To make Double Strip Heart blocks as shown in the quilt center, make 3 Flying Geese units using the (3) 5¼" × 9¾" (13.5 cm × 25 cm) pink rectangles and (6) 5¼" (13.5 cm) white background squares (follow step 3 in the Strip Heart block directions). Trim the Flying Geese units to 5" × 9½" (12.5 cm × 24 cm) (**Figure 2**).

3. Make another Flying Geese unit using the 5¼" × 9¾" (14 cm × 25 cm) blue mosaic rectangle and (2) 5¼" (13.5 cm) pink squares. Trim the Flying Geese unit to 5" × 9½" (12.5 cm × 24 cm) (**Figure 3**).

4. Following the Half-Square Triangles block directions in chapter 3, make 2 Half-Square Triangle blocks using the 5½" (14 cm) pink square and (1) 5½" (14 cm) white background square. Trim the HSTs to 5" (12.5 cm) square (**Figure 4**).

5. Pin and sew (1) 2¾" × 5" (7 cm × 12.5 cm) mustard print rectangle and (1) 2¾" × 5" (7 cm × 12.5 cm) white feather print rectangle along the longer side. Press seam open. Make 2 units (**Figure 5**).

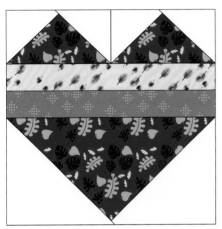

Fig. 1 **Strip Heart Block**
Make 3 blue, 4 teal, and 3 pink

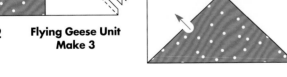

Fig. 2 **Flying Geese Unit**
Make 3

Fig. 3 **Flying Geese Unit**
Make 1

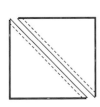

5" (14.5 cm)

5" (14.5 cm)

Fig. 4 **Half-Square Triangles**
Make 2

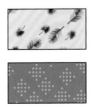

Fig. 5 **Make 2**

6. Make two Flying Geese units using the 3" × 5¼" (7.5 cm × 13.5 cm) blue mosaic rectangles and (4) 3" (7.5 cm) white feather print squares. Trim Flying Geese units to 2¾" × 5" (7 cm × 12.5 cm) (**Figure 6**).

7. Pin and sew the Flying Geese units from step 6 together at the short ends with right sides together, pressing the seam open. Sew the Flying Geese units to the 2¾" × 9½" (7 cm × 24 cm) blue mosaic strip.

8. Gather the pieces from steps 2–7 with (2) 5" (12.5 cm) white squares and arrange as shown (**Figure 7**).

9. Pin and sew the pieces together by row, pressing seams open. Sew the rows together to complete the Double Strip Heart block (**Figure 8**). Repeat steps 2–9 to make a second

Double Strip Heart block using the blue print and green spot fabrics.

10. Referring to **Figure 9**, arrange each of the Strip Heart and Double Strip Heart blocks as shown. Pin and sew the blocks together by row, taking your time to match up the points. Press seams open. Continue pinning and sewing the long rows together, pressing the seams open as you go.

11. Layer the backing (wrong-side up), the batting, and the quilt top (right-side up); baste the layers together. Quilt as desired. (The featured quilt was professionally longarm quilted.)

12. Bind the quilt. (For tips and detailed directions on finishing your quilt, see chapter 1.)

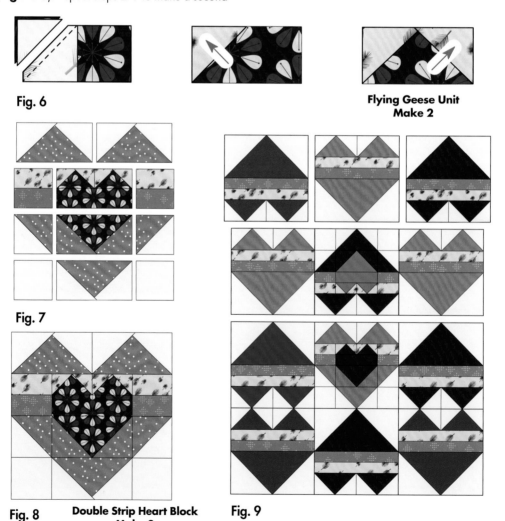

Fig. 6

**Flying Geese Unit
Make 2**

Fig. 7

Fig. 8   **Double Strip Heart Block
Make 2**

Fig. 9

MOSAIC Quilt

This fresh-looking design plays on light and shadows to make its mark. Using one colorway against a white background will give you a look similar to mine, but this quilt would also look amazing using a fat quarter bundle of your favorite fabrics or shaded colors to create an ombre look for your quilt by shading the colors from lightest to darkest from top to bottom.

Finished Quilt Size: 54½" × 72½" (138.5 cm × 184 cm)

Finished Block Size: 18" (45.5 cm) square

FAT QUARTER FRIENDLY

Materials

- Pink and white print fabric, 6 fat quarters (each 18" × 21" [45.5 cm × 53.5 cm])

- Pink print fabrics, 6 fat quarters (each 18" × 21" [45.5 cm × 53.5 cm])

- White spot fabric, 2¾ yards (2.5 m)

- Backing fabric, 62" × 80" (157.5 cm × 203 cm)

- Binding fabric, ½ yard (45.5 cm)

- Batting, 62" × 80" (157.5 cm × 203 cm)

- Rotary cutter and self-healing mat

Cutting Instructions

From each of the pink and white fat quarters, cut:

(2) 3¾" × 7" (9.5 cm × 18 cm) rectangles

(2) 3¾" × 13½" (9.5 cm × 34.5 cm) rectangles

(2) 5½" (14 cm) squares

From each of the 6 pink prints, cut:

(1) 7" (18 cm) square

(2) 5½" (14 cm) squares

(4) 5⅜" (13.5 cm) squares; subcut on the diagonal once

From the white spot fabric, cut:

(1) 7" (18 cm) × WOF (width-of-fabric strips); subcut into (6) 7" (18 cm) squares

(7) 5½" (14 cm) × WOF strips; subcut into (24) 5½" (14 cm) squares

(4) 5⅜" (13.5 cm) × WOF strips; subcut into (24) 5⅜" (13.5 cm) squares, then subcut on the diagonal once

(8) 3¾" (9.5 cm) × WOF strips; subcut into (12) 3¾" × 7" (9.5 cm × 18 cm) rectangles and (12) 3¾" × 13½" (9.5 cm × 34.5 cm) rectangles

From the binding fabric, cut:

(7) 2½" (6.5 cm) × WOF strips

All seam allowances are ¼" (6 mm) unless otherwise noted.

1. Following the instructions in chapter 3, make 6 Mosaic blocks using the pink and white print fabric pieces (**Figure 1**). Blocks should measure 18½" (47 cm) square.

2. In the same manner as step 1, make 6 Reverse Mosaic blocks using the (2) 3¾" × 7" (9.5 cm × 18 cm) white spot rectangles, (2) 3¾" × 13½" (9.5 cm × 34.5 cm) white spot rectangles, (2) 5½" (14 cm) white spot squares together with a 7" (18 cm) pink square, (2) 5½" (14 cm) pink squares, and (4) 5⅜" (13.5 cm) pink squares, cut on the diagonal once as you did in the step above. Make 6 reverse Mosaic blocks in total (**Figure 2**). Blocks should measure 18½" (47 cm) square.

3. Arrange the 6 Mosaic blocks and 6 Reverse Mosaic blocks in a 3 × 4 pattern (see the finished quilt for reference) until you are happy with the color and print distribution.

4. Sew each of the blocks together by row, pinning to match up the points and pressing seams open.

5. Sew each of the rows together, taking your time to pin these rows and match up the points. Press the seams open. Continue sewing all the long rows together, pinning and pressing as you go.

6. Layer the backing (wrong-side up), the batting, and the quilt top (right-side up); baste the layers together. Quilt as desired. (The featured quilt was professionally longarm quilted.)

7. Bind the quilt. (For tips and detailed directions on finishing your quilt, turn to chapter 1.)

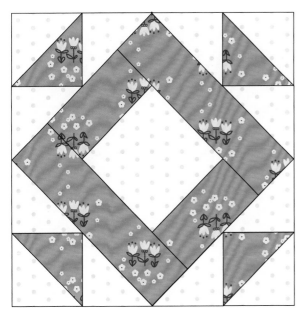

Fig. 1

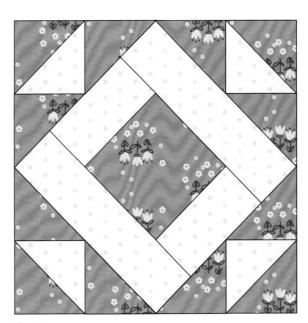

Fig. 2

INDIAN BLOCK
Table Runner

When the seasons change, it is fun to switch up the décor in your home. This graphic runner will make a bold impact on any table especially when used outdoors for summer parties with family and friends. For a different look, try using the 20" (51 cm) Rising Star block in chapter 3.

Finished Table Runner Size: 20½" × 60½" (52 cm × 153.5 cm)
Finished Block Size: 20" (51 cm)

Materials

- White fabric, ½ yard (45.5 cm)

- Black fabric, ½ yard (45.5 cm)

- Yellow fabric, 1 fat quarter (18" × 21" [45.5 cm × 53.5 cm])

- Mint fabric, ⅓ yard (30.5 cm)

- Backing fabric, 24" × 68" (61 cm × 172.5 cm)

- Binding fabric, ⅜ yard (34.5 cm)

- Batting, 24" × 68" (61 cm × 172.5 cm)

- 5½" (14 cm) Bloc Loc Half-Square Triangle Square Up Ruler (optional)

- Erasable fabric marking pen

Cutting Instructions

From the white fabric, cut:

(2) 6" (15 cm) × WOF (width-of-fabric) strips; subcut into (12) 6" (15 cm) squares

(1) 5½" (14 cm) × WOF strip; subcut into (6) 5½" (14 cm) squares

From the black fabric, cut:

(2) 6" (15 cm) × WOF strips; subcut into (12) 6" (15 cm) squares

(1) 5½" (14 cm) × WOF strip; subcut into (6) 5½" (14 cm) squares

From the yellow fabric, cut:

(1) 10½" (26.5 cm) square

From the mint fabric, cut:

(2) 10½" (26.5 cm) squares

From the binding fabric, cut:

(5) 2½" (6.5 cm) × WOF strips

All seam allowances are ¼" (6 mm) unless otherwise indicated.

1. Following the Indian block instructions in chapter 3, make 1 yellow Indian block and 2 mint Indian blocks.

2. Arrange the Indian blocks with the yellow block in the center and the mint blocks either side as shown (**Figure 1**).

3. With right sides together, pin and sew the Indian blocks together along the sides, pressing seams open.

4. Layer the backing (wrong-side up), the batting, and the table runner top (right-side up); baste the layers together. Quilt as desired. (The featured runner was machine quilted with diagonal lines along the HSTs. I also used the horizontal lines to sew in the ditch.)

5. Bind the Table Runner. (For tips and detailed directions on finishing your table runner, to turn chapter 1.)

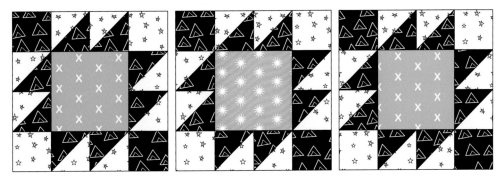

Fig. 1

Working with Directional Fabrics

I used a directional fabric for the black fabric. Directional fabrics can be tricky to work as the pattern can become distorted and may not look as you imagined once it has been cut up and sewn into different directions. However, in this design you are able to turn the blocks and HSTs, which makes working with the directional fabric easier. When you are arranging your blocks, turn the fabric and match up the pattern together with those blocks that run in the correct direction. This will give your project a cohesive and balanced look. If you are working on a project where the directional fabric can't be turned around due to the block construction, it may be worthwhile to buy a little extra fabric so you have the option of adjusting the cutting and placement of your directional fabric.

SCRAPPY HALF-SQUARE TRIANGLE

Pillow

When making big blocks, there can be leftover trimmings that are larger than what you may be used to. This scrap-busting project has been designed to use these trimmings so you can make a pillow to coordinate with your quilt. You can put all those leftover half triangles to good use in this pillow. Alternatively, you can make this pillow from a fat eighth bundle and some background fabric, or dive into your scrap basket and use some of those pieces up. Additional projects with trimmings that are big enough for this pillow include the Flying Geese Quilt, Lozenge Quilt, Strip Heart Quilt, and Constellation Sampler Quilt.

Finished Pillow Size: 24" (61 cm) square

Alternative Designs

Using these directions, you can make several blocks and join them together to make a stunning quilt. You'll need nine blocks for a lap quilt, while twelve blocks will make a beautiful bed-sized quilt.

Materials
* (from leftover trimmings)

◢ *Note: If you are buying fabric for this pillow instead of using trimmings, see No Scraps? No Problem for fabric requirements and cutting directions.*

- Print triangles (large), 8 measuring at least 7" (18 cm) on the two short sides

- Print triangles (small), 32 measuring at least 4" (10 cm) on the two short sides

- Background fabric triangles (large), 8 measuring at least 7" (18 cm) on the two short sides

- Background fabric triangles (small), 32 measuring at least 4" (10 cm) on the two short sides

- Backing fabric, ¾ yard (68.5 cm)

- Batting, 30" (76 cm)

- Pillow insert, 26" (61 cm) (I used the large Ikea pillows)

- Zipper, 24" (61 cm)

- 6½" (16.5 cm) and 3½" (9 cm) Bloc Loc Half-Square Triangle Square Up Rulers (optional)

- Erasable fabric marking pen

- Zipper foot

Cutting Instructions

From the backing fabric, cut:

(1) 9" × 24½" (23 cm × 62 cm) rectangle

(1) 18" × 24½" (45.5 cm × 62 cm) rectangle

All seam allowances are ¼" (6 mm) unless otherwise noted.

◢ **No Scraps? No Problem.**

If you don't have enough fabric trimmings left over from another project to make this pillow, here's what you will need to do to make this project with new fabric.

MATERIALS

Print fabrics, 10 fat eighths (each 9" × 21" [23 cm × 53.5 cm])

Background fabric, ½ yard (45.5 cm)

CUTTING DIRECTIONS

From print squares, cut:

(4) 7" (18 cm) squares

(16) 4" (10 cm) squares

From background fabric, cut:

(4) 7" (18 cm) squares

(16) 4" (10 cm) squares

Using the HST instructions in chapter 3, make (8) 6½" (16.5 cm) HSTs and (32) small 3½" (9 cm) HSTs. Follow steps 3–9 to finish the pillow.

1. Make 8 large Half-Square Triangles (HSTs) from the larger triangles left over from your project. Place a large print triangle and a large background fabric triangle right sides together. Sew along the diagonal of the two triangles (**Figure 1**). Press the seam toward the darker fabric and trim to 6½" (16.5 cm) square (**Figure 2**).

2. In the same manner as step 1, make (32) 3½" (9 cm) HSTs with the smaller print triangle trimmings and smaller background triangles.

3. Arrange 4 small HSTs as shown (**Figure 3**). Pin and sew the HSTs together by row, pressing the seam from each row in alternate directions. Pin and sew the top and bottom row together (**Figure 4**). Press the seams open. The unit should measure 6½" (16.5 cm) unfinished. Make 8 units total.

4. Arrange the large HSTs and the HST units together as shown (**Figure 5**).

5. Referring to **Figure 6**, pin and sew the blocks together in each row, pressing the seams open.

6. Pin and sew each of the rows together, taking your time to match up the points. Press the seams open. Continue sewing the long rows together, pinning and pressing as you go.

7. Layer the batting and pillow top (right-side up); baste them together. Quilt as desired. (The featured design was machine quilted with diagonal lines along the print HSTs.) Trim the batting and pillow top to 24½" (62 cm) square.

8. Add a zipper backing following steps 3–8 in the Home and Hearth Pillow.

9. Turn the pillow right-side out and fill with the insert.

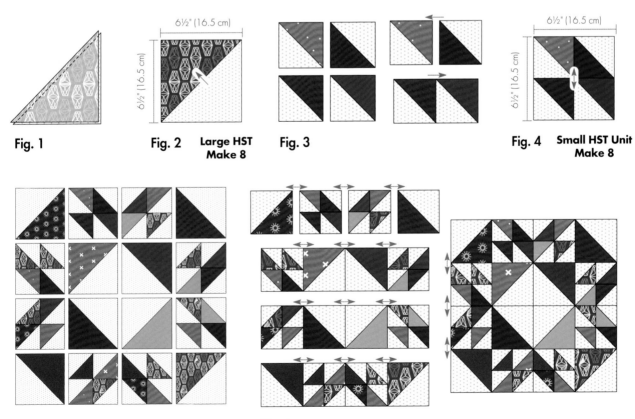

Fig. 1

6½" (16.5 cm) 6½" (16.5 cm)

Fig. 2 **Large HST Make 8**

Fig. 3

6½" (16.5 cm) 6½" (16.5 cm)

Fig. 4 **Small HST Unit Make 8**

Fig. 5

Fig. 6

CHAPTER 5

QUILT BACKINGS

For me, the back of a quilt is never "just the back." So much effort, time, fabric, money, and love go into the front that I like to put plenty of thought into the backing as well, making it the perfect finishing touch to a quilt. With a little planning, the backing can be an important part of the design and make your quilt even more versatile.

This is different for every quilt, of course. Sometimes we want a quick present and the backing fabric may be something we have on hand that ties in beautifully with the front. If you are making crib-sized quilts, for example, small quantities of yardage may work well in this instance.

When it comes to lap, bed, or larger sized quilts, there are plenty of options to fancy up the back. Some are quicker than others, as with wide-back fabric options, while others may be pieced in as many pieces as the front, taking more time but providing big impact for the finished quilt.

Often we have "orphan blocks" or spare blocks made from the quilt top fabrics. Incorporating orphan blocks into a pieced backing is a great way to give them a "home," and using spare blocks from the quilt top will tie together the front and back of your quilt.

Backing Options

There are several different fabric options for the back of a quilt.

WIDE-BACK FABRICS

These backing fabrics are 108" (274.5 cm) wide. They usually come on a large roll or bolt, and you can use them for larger quilts without having to piece fabric together. They usually have simpler patterns and while they are cheaper than quilting cotton (the fabric you would use for the front), the quality and variety is always improving. Not only do wide-back fabrics come in cotton, these days there are also sateen and voile options available from popular designers.

QUILTING COTTON

This is the regular quilting cotton fabric you buy for your quilt top that is 42" (106.5 cm) wide. If you are making smaller projects like cushions, runners or lap quilts, you generally may not need to piece these fabrics. However, for larger quilting projects you may need to join these by machine piecing two lengths together.

I often make kids' quilts and projects. The backing can add lots of fun by using a complementary novelty fabric on the back to tie in with the design on the front.

Fabrics with big bold patterns in them, such as floral prints or geometric designs, can also be great to complement the front of a quilt. If you are using a set fabric range in your project, you may want to choose one of the main prints to use as backing fabric or any of the coordinating prints from the range to finish off your quilt. Check out the "sale" fabrics in your local quilting or fabric store as well. These fabrics can be great to pick up in bulk quantities and are perfect to save to use for a backing at a great price.

I also like to use different substrate options for backings as well. Lawn is perfect for backing because the fabrics are lightweight, have a beautiful soft drape to them, and come in a great variety of prints and colors. Chambray is also lightweight enough for a backing. It will give more structure to your quilt and can really show off the finished machine or hand quilting.

Flannel or minky are poplar choices to use for backs with quilts that have flannel in the quilt top. Flannel or minky are soft and cuddly, warm and provide an added textural element to your quilt. Wide-back options are now available as well.

SHEETS

Buying bed sheets for the back of your quilt is another option. You may need to experiment a little with the quality of the sheet if you are looking to use this. A sheet is nice and wide so it doesn't require joining for larger projects but the thread count can sometimes cause an issue, so always test the quality first before beginning the process of basting your quilt.

HOW MUCH BACKING DO I BUY?

When it comes to purchasing fabric for the back of your quilt, you need the measurements of your finished quilt top. When you know the complete size of the quilt top, add 4" (10 cm) to each width and length of your quilt top. For example, if your quilt top measures 60" × 80" (152.5 cm × 203 cm) you will need to purchase 68" × 88" (172.5 cm × 223.5 cm) of backing fabric.

LONGARM QUILTING REQUIREMENTS

If you are having your quilt quilted by a professional longarm quilter and you are planning on a pieced back, always have a chat with your quilter first. My longarm quilter prefers any seam on a pieced backing to be pressed open. This ensures that seams are nice and flat and don't cause any issues, as they can't be seen while quilting.

How to Piece a Quilt Back

When piecing fabric together, cut off the selvedges and pin the right sides together. Sew using a ½" (1.3 cm) seam allowance and press your seam open.

PATTERN MATCHING

When you are joining 42" (106.5 cm) quilting cotton, especially a busy or large-print fabric, pattern matching the joining seam will result in a better-looking back. If the pattern is a busy small floral or a polka dot, then I usually don't pattern match these types of prints. However, if you are using a large 1" (2.5 cm) spot print, floral, novelty, or check print, for example, then it is worth joining the fabric pieces by pattern matching to give a professional finish to your quilt backing. While it takes longer and requires more fabric, the result is always worth the extra effort and time.

When you are purchasing 42" (106.5 cm) fabric, you will first need to decide if the print is directional. Determine which way the direction of the fabric runs and how you want it to run in your quilt top. Then purchase fabric according to the length or width of your fabric, depending on the direction of the print.

Pattern matching usually requires the purchase of additional yardage. This is to allow for matching up where the pattern runs so that you can line up the pattern with the pattern repeat in the print of the fabric. I will usually buy between ⅓–½ yard (30.5–45.5 cm) extra, depending on the size of the pattern repeat to allow for pattern matching of my backing fabric.

Pieced Backing Ideas

There are lots of reasons to piece a backing fabric. Maybe you can't find the right color or print in a wide-back fabric, maybe you would like to give those spare blocks a home, and sometimes it is a great way to use hoarded fabric in your stash. Maybe it is the perfect print to finish off your quilt or you may have offcuts left over from other wide-back fabrics that you have used in previous quilts. Piecing your backing is a fantastic way to put these types of fabrics to good use.

On the following pages are some ideas and inspiration to piece backing fabrics together.

◢ Pattern Matching 42" (106.5 cm) Fabric

1. Measure the quilt top. Cut your first length of 42" (106.5 cm) backing fabric at least 8" (20.5 cm) longer than your quilt top. Do not cut your second piece of 42" (106.5 cm) quilting fabric as this is the piece you will use to line up the pattern.

2. Cut the selvedges off the first backing fabric piece.

3. Measure and fold over ½" (1.3 cm) of the raw long edge of your first cut length of backing fabric. Press this fold.

◢ *Note: If you are using a check print, fold back a full check.*

4. Lay the second backing piece (the longer one) on your work surface, then using your first piece, line up the fold on the pattern repeat. It may take a little time to find the repeat, but the extra fabric on the second piece means you can move the first piece forward or sideways until you have it in the correct position.

5. Once you have the pattern lined up, open out the folded edge of your first piece and pin the seam in place along the folded line. Pin generously.

6. Sew along the pressed fold line of your backing fabric, removing the pins before you come to them. Take time to ensure your seam is nice and straight.

7. Trim back the seam to ½" (1.3 cm) and press the seam open.

Strip Heart Quilt Backing

Refer to **Figure 1** throughout assembly.

Backing Size: 62" x 80½" (157.5 cm x 204.5 cm)

Materials

- Blue check fabric (59" [150 cm]) wide), 3 yards (2.8 m)

- Leftover corner trimmings from your project

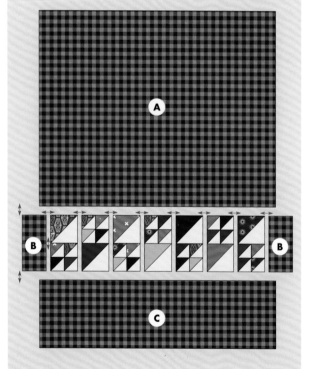

CUTTING INSTRUCTIONS

From the blue check fabric cut:

(1) 62" × 49½" (157.5 cm x 125.5 cm) from the LOF (length-of-fabric) for piece A

(2) 17½" (44.5 cm) × WOF (width-of-fabric) strips

(2) 6¾" × 14½" (17 cm x 37 cm) rectangles for piece B

All seam allowances are ¼" (6 mm) unless otherwise noted.

1. Using the leftover corner trimmings from the Strip Heart Quilt in chapter 4 and following the Half-Square Triangle instructions in chapter 3, make (28) 4" (10 cm) small Half-Square Triangles (HSTs) and (7) 7½" (19 cm) large HSTs. Press all the seams open.

2. Sew the small HSTs together in groups of four. Pressing seams open so that each block of four measures 7½" (19 cm). Make 7 units total.

3. Arrange the small and large HSTs in pairs as shown. Pin and sew these rows together, pressing seams open as you go.

4. Sew the (2) 17½" (44.5 cm) × WOF strips together along the 17½" (44.5 cm) width to make piece C. Press the seam open and cut the piece to measure 17½" × 60" (44.5 cm x 152.5 cm).

5. Arrange the backing fabric pieces as shown.

6. Sew a piece C rectangle to either side of the Pieced Half-Square Triangle unit. Press the seams open. Sew pieces A and C to this pieced center as shown. Press all seams open.

Half-Square Triangles Quilt Back

Refer to **Figure 1** throughout assembly.

Backing Size: 80" (203 cm) square

Materials

- Print fabrics, 10 (each approximately 10" [25.5 cm] square)

- Pink fabric, 2¼ yards (2 m)

- Floral print fabric, 2¼ yards (2 m)

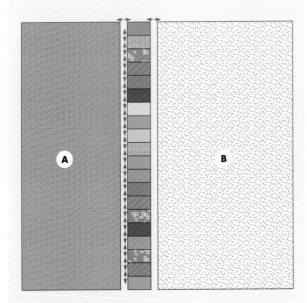

From the print fabrics, cut:

(20) 4½" × 7½" (11.5 cm × 19 cm) rectangles

From the pink fabric, cut:

(1) 31" × 80" (78.5 cm × 203 cm) rectangle for piece A

From the floral fabric, cut:

(1) 42" × 80" (106.5 cm × 203 cm) rectangle for piece B

All seam allowances are ¼" (6 mm) unless otherwise noted.

1. Arrange the 4½" × 7 ½" (11.5 cm × 19 cm) printed fabric rectangles in a long strip.

2. Pin and sew the rectangles together to make one long strip, sewing each rectangle with right sides facing along the 7½" (19 cm) side to the next rectangle. Press the seams open.

3. Pin and sew pink piece A to the left side of the pieced rectangles. Press the seams open.

4. Pin and sew floral piece B to the right side of the pieced rectangles. Press seams open.

Log Cabin Quilt Back

Refer to **Figure 1** throughout assembly.

Backing Size: 70½" × 80½" (179 cm × 204.5 cm)

Materials

- Purple fabric, 1¼ yard (1.1 m)

- Peach fabric, 1¼ yard (1.1 m)

- Blue fabric, 1¼ yard (1.1 m)

- Yellow fabric, 1¼ yard (1.1 m)

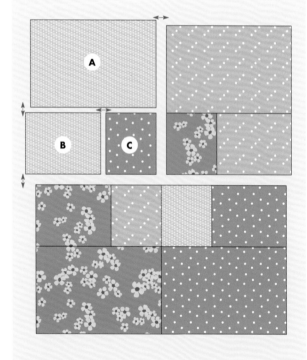

CUTTING INSTRUCTIONS

From each of the purple, peach, blue, and yellow fabrics, cut:

(1) 14½" × 17" (37 cm × 43 cm) rectangle for piece C

(1) 17" × 21½" (43 cm × 54.5 cm) rectangle for piece B

(1) 24" × 35½" (61 cm × 90 cm) rectangle for piece A

All seam allowances are ¼" (6 mm) unless otherwise indicated.

1. Lay out and arrange your blocks as shown.

2. Pin the contrasting color piece C and piece B with right sides together along the 17" (43 cm) length and sew. Press seams open. Repeat for the 3 remaining center blocks.

3. Pin and sew the matching piece A to the top or bottom of each center block.

4. Pin and sew the first row, pressing seams open. Pin and sew the second row, pressing seams open.

5. Pin and sew the first and second rows together to complete your quilt back. Press the seams open.

Simplex Star Back

▲ *Note: Any of the 24" (61 cm) finished blocks are interchangeable into this backing.*

Backing Size: 104" (264 cm) square

Materials

- Gray fabric (at least 59" [150 cm] wide), 6 yards (5.5 m)

- Simplex Star block (see chapter 3)

▲ *Note: Due to the large size of this quilt, when using a pieced backing it is recommended that you buy 59" (150 cm) wide fabric to allow for minimal waste and less piecing.*

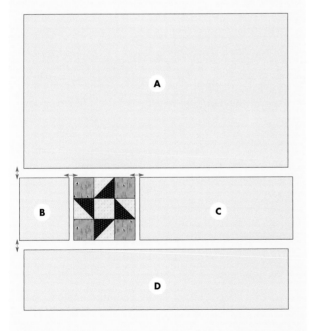

CUTTING INSTRUCTIONS

From the length of gray fabric, cut:

(1) 59½" × 104" (151 cm × 264 cm) strip for piece A

(1) 20" × 24½" (51 cm × 62 cm) strip for piece B

(1) 24½" × 60½" (62 cm × 153.5 cm) strip for piece C

(1) 21" × 104" (53.5 cm × 264 cm) strip for piece D

All seam allowances are ¼" (6 mm) unless otherwise indicated.

1. Make a Simplex Star block according to the instructions in chapter 3.

2. Referring to **Figure 1**, pin together the piece B to one side of the Simplex Star block; machine sew and then press seam open. Sew piece C to the other side of the Simplex Star block; press seam open.

3. Sew the piece A to the top of the Simplex Star strip. Pin carefully along this long length. Press seams open. Repeat for sewing piece D to the bottom of the Simplex Star strip.

Churn Dash Quilt Back

Refer to **Figure 1** throughout assembly.

Backing Size: 64½" (164 cm) square

Materials

- Multicolor print fabric, 3¼ yards (3 m)
- White/gold spot fabric, ⅞ yard (80 cm)
- Erasable fabric marking pen

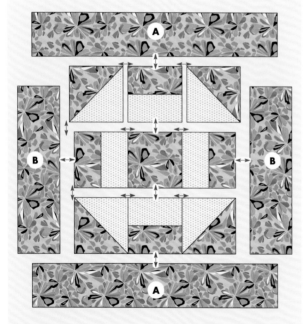

CUTING INSTRUCTIONS

From the multicolor print fabric, cut:

(2) 11½" × 64½" (29 cm × 164 cm) LOF (length-of-fabric) border strips for piece A

(2) 11½" × 42½" (29 cm × 108 cm) LOF border strips for piece B

(2) 15" (38 cm) squares

(1) 14½" (37 cm) square

(4) 7½" × 14½" (19 cm × 37 cm) rectangles

From the white/gold spot fabric, cut:

(2) 15" (38 cm) squares

(4) 7½" × 14½" (19 cm × 37 cm) rectangles

All seam allowances are ¼" (6 mm) unless otherwise indicated.

1. Following the instructions in chapter 3, make a Churn Dash block using the (2) 15" (38 cm) multicolor print squares, (1) 14½" (37 cm) multicolor print square, (4) 7½" × 14½" (19 cm × 37 cm) multicolor print rectangles, (2) 15" (38 cm) white/gold squares, and (4) 7½" × 14½" (19 cm × 37 cm) white/gold rectangles. Trim the HST to 14½" (37 cm) square. Press all seams open.

2. Pin 1 piece B to both the left and right sides of the center Churn Dash block with right sides together and sew. Press the seams open.

3. In the same manner, pin and sew 1 piece A to the top and bottom of the Churn Dash center block. Press the seams open.

ACKNOWLEDGMENTS

Such a big thank you to Carol Brady from The Quilting Cottage. You have spent so much time and effort working on the quilting of these quilts in this book, and I could not be more thrilled with how they have turned out. Thank you!

To Alisha at Ministry of Fabric for supplying and providing fabric to use in the projects—you were always happy to send what I needed.

Cotton+Steel, Ella Blue Fabrics, Fat Quarter Shop, and Aurifil: You have been so supportive with supplying fabrics and notions, and I am very grateful to you all for working with me on this.

Thank you also to Victorian Textiles for providing the Matilda's Own Batting and to Bloc-Loc for sending me the supersized rulers, which made the projects a breeze.

To my editor, Jodi Butler, I could not have done this without your support, guidance, and encouragement.

Most of all to my family, Ronny and my two girls, Shayla and Ashlyn. This book has been a massive undertaking and you have been there each step of the way.

Metric Conversion Chart

TO CONVERT	TO	MULTIPLY BY
Inches	Centimeters	2.54
Centimeters	Inches	0.4
Feet	Centimeters	30.5
Centimeters	Feet	0.03
Yards	Meters	0.9
Meters	Yards	1.1

ABOUT THE AUTHOR

Jemima Flendt is a professional quiltmaker and sewing pattern designer based in Perth, Western Australia. She is passionate about teaching quilting and sewing to others, especially beginners, due to her background as a home economics teacher. Jemima contributes to publications worldwide as well as teaching and filming quilting classes internationally.

Jemima's first book, *Weekend Quilting*, has been a big hit, proving you can quilt and sew even in a short amount of time. Now she's back, taking your quilting to the next level by showing you how to make big blocks for fast finishes. Visit Jemima at www.tiedwitharibbon.com.

RESOURCES

Quilting

The Quilting Cottage
www.carolbradyquilting.blogspot.com.au

Supplies and Fabric

Ministry of Fabric
www.ministryoffabric.com.au

Fat Quarter Shop
www.fatquartershop.com

Cotton+Steel
www.cottonandsteelfabrics.com

Notions

Aurifil Thread
www.aurifil.com

Bloc Loc Rulers
www.blocloc.com

Matilda's Own Batting
www.victoriantextiles.com.au

Quilt Pantographs

Carol Brady
www.carolbradyquilting.blogspot.com.au

Anita Shakelford
www.anitashackelford.net

Karlee Porter
www.karleeporter.com

Sharon Perry
www.houseofcreations.biz

Patricia Ritter
www.urbanelementz.com

INDEX

WHAT ARE YOU MAKING NEXT?

Check out these great titles from The Quilting Company.

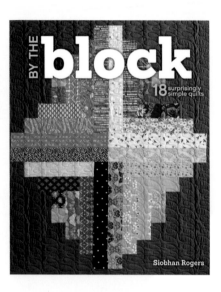